böhlau

Ryan Hugh Ross

JULIUS BÜRGER

Composer – Conductor – Vocal Coach

Gerold Gruber (Ed.)

Böhlau

Exilarte Zentrum der mdw – Universität für Musik und darstellende Kunst Wien
Ryan Hugh Ross, Gerold Gruber (Ed.)
Julius Bürger. Composer – Conductor – Vocal Coach

Bibliografische Information der Deutschen Nationalbibliothek :
Die Deutsche Nationalbibliothek verzeichnet diese Publikation
in der Deutschen Nationalbibliografie ; detaillierte bibliografische
Daten sind im Internet über http://dnb.d-nb.de abrufbar.

© 2024 Böhlau, Zeltgasse 1, A-1080 Wien, ein Imprint der Brill-Gruppe
(Koninklijke Brill NV, Leiden, Niederlande; Brill USA Inc., Boston MA, USA; Brill Asia Pte Ltd, Singapore;
Brill Deutschland GmbH, Paderborn, Deutschland ; Brill Österreich GmbH, Wien, Österreich)
Koninklijke Brill NV umfasst die Imprints Brill, Brill Nijhoff, Brill Hotei, Brill Schöningh,
Brill Fink, Brill mentis, Vandenhoeck & Ruprecht, Böhlau und V&R unipress.
Alle Rechte vorbehalten. Das Werk und seine Teile sind urheberrechtlich geschützt.
Jede Verwertung in anderen als den gesetzlich zugelassenen Fällen bedarf der vorherigen schriftlichen Einwilligung des Verlages.

Gestaltung Layout und Satz; Lektorat: Iby-Jolande Varga
Umschlagfotos: © A-Weaz
Druck und Bindung: Finidr, Český Těšín
Printed in the EU

Vandenhoeck & Ruprecht Verlage | www.vandenhoeck-ruprecht-verlage.com
ISBN 978-3-205-22074-9

CONTENTS

1. Introduction	7
2. Julius Burger's biography	
2.1 Vienna period (1897–1919)	8
2.2 Berlin period (1919–1933)	11
2.2.1. Apprenticeship at the Metropolitan Opera, New York	13
2.2.2. Return to Berlin	14
2.3 London period (1934–1939)	17
2.4 New York period (1939–1995)	28
3. Julius Burger's opus	
3.1 Instrumental Music	
3.1.1 Chamber music	45
3.1.2 Orchestral works	47
3.2 Vocal Music	
3.2.1 Voice and Piano	56
3.2.2 Voice and Orchestra	70
3.2.3 Choral Works	77
3.3 Sketches and others	
3.3.1. Works for stage	80
3.4 Radio Music	85
4. Conclusion	101
Estate Julius Bürger	103
Photo Credits	110

Julius Burger (Bürger) in the early 1930s © A-Weaz

1. INTRODUCTION

This research focuses on the life and work of Julius Burger (Bürger), a Viennese born composer whose long and varied career intersected with many important European and American musical figures and institutions of the 20th Century. Despite his large œuvre and interesting life, little to no musicological research has been conducted on Julius Burger to date. Thus, the main objective of this paper is to provide an overview of the composer's biography, as well as key aspects of his œuvre, utilising his estate as a basis. The paper is not intended as a comprehensive reconstruction of said works but rather as a starting point for future studies of Julius Burger's œuvre utilising documentation of composer's estate preserved in the Exilarte Archiv der mdw, Vienna.

Julius Burger's life and work would have been lost to history without the care and dedication of his friend, attorney Ronald S. Pohl, Esq. Through Pohl's efforts, a large portion of Burger's music was premiered through numerous concert performances in the early 1990s. Selections from the composer's orchestral works were also recorded for commercial release which aided in the composer's rediscovery. After Burger's death in 1995, Pohl continued to preserve and promote the unpublished compositions until installing the estate on permanent loan with the Exilarte centre at the Vienna University of Music and Performing Arts, in the same building where Burger began his studies. A noteworthy concert in promotion of Burger's works includes the 18 August 2023 Austrian premiere of selections from the composer's orchestral œuvre-marking his spiritual return to Vienna 85 years after his exile began in 1938. The estate includes Burger's compositions in autograph manuscript form as well as a large collection of personal documents and papers, recordings, newspaper articles and photographs.

While research has revealed numerous examples of Burger's works having been broadcast in the 1930s and 1940s (Berlin and London) as well as several recorded works, only one known work, *Launisches Glück*, was published in the composer's lifetime. Additionally, relatively few selections from his concert œuvre received performances until the 1990s. Thus, this paper has relied on documentation from Julius Burger's estate preserved at the Exilarte Zentrum Archiv der mdw, Vienna as well as other archival repositories including the Archiv der Universität Wien, the Universitätsarchiv – Universität der Künste Berlin, the BBC Written Archives Centre – Caversham, England, the BBC Sheet Music Library – Perivale, England and the New York Public Library Archives – New York, NY. Additional information has been procured from private collections, among others.

These materials provide a wealth of insight into Julius Burger's storied career as a composer, conductor, arranger and repetiteur which spanned over seven decades in respected institutions throughout Europe and the United States.

2. JULIUS BURGER'S BIOGRAPHY

Julius Burger's biography can be roughly divided into four periods: the Vienna period (1897–1919), the Berlin period (1919–1933), the initial exile period deemed the London period (1933–1939) and the New York period (1939–1995).

2.1 Vienna period (1897–1919)

Julius Burger was born on 11 March 1897 in Vienna's 2nd District of Leopoldstadt, the fifth child of nine to Josef Bürger – a tailor – and Chaje (Clara) Bürger – a homemaker. Josef, born under the reign of Emperor Franz Joseph in 1859, was born in the village of Olejów in the Kingdom of Galicia while Chaje originated from the town of Kamionka Strumiłowa in Galicia (now Kamianka-Buzka in modern Ukraine). While little is known about Julius Burger's early life, the main record of this period stems from an interview with his family friend, Dr. Trude Zörer. Early in the interview, Julius recollected his childhood as being "carefree." She notes father Josef's work provided adequate financial means for the large family. Equally, Burger's parents put a strong emphasis on education and each child was afforded the opportunity to study.[1]

According to Burger, his love affair with music began when, as a toddler, he encountered a Werkelmann (Leierkastenmann). He was fascinated by the tones emanating from the hand-cranked instrument and followed the performer through the city until he was eventually retrieved by a family member in the 19th district.[2] As an adolescent, Burger was admitted to the Kaiserlich-Königliches Erzherzog-Rainer-Gymnasium where he studied from 1908 until the summer of 1913. The Gymnasium (renamed in 1989 after former pupil Sigmund Freud) was located in the 2nd district.[3] Other noteworthy former pupils include anatomist Julius Tandler (1869–1936), and neurologist, psychiatrist and founder of Logotherapy Victor Emil Frankl (1905–1997).[4]

Burger continued his studies at the Kaiserlich-Königliches Maximilian-Gymnasium (Wasagymnasium) in Vienna's 9th district until completion in 1916.[5] The prestigious institution served as one of the prime educational centres for children of Vienna's cultivated Jewish bourgeoisie in the early twenti-

---

1   Julius Burger, "Julius Burger speaks to Trude Zörer on his friendship with Joseph Schmidt," interview by Dr. Trude Zörer, date of recording unknown, audio, 24:22, from the private collection of Dr. Trude Zörer.
2   Dr. Trude Zörer, "Interview by Ryan Hugh Ross on the life of Julius Burger (Bürger)," Question No. 4, 30 October 2019.
3   Walter Jahn, "Geschichte des Sigmund Freud-Gymnasiums," Sigmund Freud Gymnasium website, URL: https://www.freudgymnasium.at/index.php/schulorganisation/geschichte , Accessed 19 November 2021.
4   Ibid.
5   Reifezeugnis, issued by Prüfungs-Kommission für K.K. Franz Joseph Real Gymnasium, 31 July 1916, Julius Burger Collection, Exilarte Zentrum Archiv der mdw, Vienna, Austria. Accessed 31 October 2018.

Enrollment Document for Julius Bürger
Archiv der Universität Wien, Nationale von Julius Bürger, Philosophische Fakultät, Wintersemester 1916/17

eth century.⁶ Examples of the Gymnasium's illustrious alumni include writer Felix Braun (1885–1973) and composer Max Deutsch (1892–1982) as well as many influential émigrés including conductor Kurt Adler 1907–1977), composer Hans Gál (1890–1987), composer and musicologist Wilhelm Grosz (1894–1939), conductors Erich Kleiber (1890–1956) and Josef Krips (1902–1974) and writer Stefan Zweig (1881–1942). Zweig detailed his experiences at the Gymnasium in his posthumous autobiographical work Die *Welt von Gestern* (1942).⁷ While still a student at the illustrious Gymnasium, Burger composed his first work in 1915, a lied setting of Heinrich Heine's *Dämmernd liegt der Sommerabend*.⁸

Although it was evident the young Burger had a fine singing voice (which he maintained throughout his life), he selected music composition as his career focus and commenced formal study at the Faculty of Arts, University of Vienna in autumn 1916. He continued at the University until summer 1917.⁹ According to his registration documents, Burger attended lectures with one of the founders of the discipline of musicology, Dr Guido Adler (1855–1941), as well as Austrian (later British) composer and musicologist Egon Wellesz (1885–1974). Other lectures were proctored by renowned educators such as Richard Wallaschek (1860–1917), Hermann Grädener (1844–1929), Wilhelm Fischer (1886–1962) and Robert Reininger (1869–1955).¹⁰

In the autumn of 1917, he began studies at the Akademie für Musik und darstellende Kunst, Wien (now Universität) where he undertook practical study in harmony and piano and participated in the choral school. In his second academic year at the academy, Burger also added piano accompaniment and lessons on the cello to his workload. Most notably, he also began studies in composition and counterpoint with renowned Austrian composer Franz Schreker (1878–1934).¹¹ Schreker's influence on Burger's compositional style is readily apparent and was defined by this important relationship.

Aside from his formal studies, Burger was employed as a keyboard accompanist in some of Vienna's silent film theatres. The exposure to these accompaniment practices and their similarities to pastiche musical repertoire of early-twentieth-century operetta provide one possible inspiration for Burger's later Radio Potpourri creations. During this period he also found employment as an accompanist to Moravian tenor Leo Slezak (1873–1946) on concert tour.¹²

---

6   Marsha L. Rosenblit, *The Jews of Vienna, 1867–1914: Assimilation and Identity* (Albany, NY: State University of New York Press, 1983), p.108-114.

7   Stefan Zweig, "Die Schule im vorigen Jahrhundert," from *Die Welt von Gestern: Erinnerungen eines Europäers* (Stockholm: Bermann-Fischer Verlag, 1942).

8   Heinrich Heine, 'Dämmernd liegt der Sommerabend (LXXXV)' in *Die Heimkehr* from *Buch der Lieder* (Hamburg: Hoffmann and Campe, 1827).

9   Enrollment documents for Julius Bürger from the Archiv der Universität Wien, Winter 1916/1917, p.119-121 and Summer 1917, p.089.

10   Ibid.

11   Julius Bürger, Enrollment document from Akademie für Musik und darstellende Kunst Wien, Matrikel Nr.(285), 1917/18; 1918/19.

12   Malcolm MacDonald, "Julius Burger (1897–1995): Orchestral Music," Liner Notes, Radio Symphonie Orchester, Berlin, cond. Simone Young, recorded 26–28,30 September 1994, Toccata Classics, TOCC 0001, 2007, CD, p.3.

2.2 Berlin period (1919–1933)

Burger left his studies with Schreker at the Universität für Musik Wien in 1919 and enrolled at the Hochschule für Musik Berlin to continue his composition studies with German composer Engelbert Humperdinck (1854–1921). However, Burger's study under the composer of *Hansel und Gretel* lasted only until the Easter of 1920 as Humperdinck's teaching was already limited due to continued illness. During this period, Burger married Olga Emma Fechner in the summer of 1920.[13] Little is known about this marriage although it represents the first of three marriages between 1920 and 1933.

In spring of 1920, it was announced that Franz Schreker had been appointed director of the Berlin Musikhochschule. This prompted Burger to return to Vienna where he rejoined his former teacher's studio and readied preparations for a more permanent move to Berlin in the Autumn of 1920. Other Schreker students who followed to Berlin included Alfred Freudenheim (1898–1941), Alois Hába (1893–1973), Jascha Horenstein (1898–1973), Ernst Krenek (1900–1991), Alois Melichar (1896–1976), Karol Rathaus (1895–1954) and Isaak Thaler (b.1902–?).[14] Schreker discouraged imitation of his own compositional idiom, opting instead to encourage each student to develop their own individual style. This contributed to an environment in which the students excelled. Their skills were not lost on the examination committee at the Berlin Musikhochschule, including Georg Schünemann, who mused on his first interactions with the students for a 1928 issue of the music journal *Anbruch*.[15]

One aspect of Schreker's new approach to the curriculum included regular performances of works by the composition students for one another in a concert setting. One such performance, on 18 June 1921, featured Burger's *Doppelfuge für Zwei Klaviere* (now lost) alongside works by Ernst Krenek (*Sonate fis-Moll für Violine und Klavier* and *Serenade für Klarinette, Violine, Bratsche und Violincello*), Alois Hába (*Quartett für Zwei Violinen Bratsche und Violincello*) and Paul Höffer (1895–1949) (*Sonate in E-Dur für Klavier*).[16]

---

13   Heiratsliste für Julius Bürger und Olga Emma Fechner, 8 June 1920, Heiratsregister der Berliner Standesämter 1874–1936, Landesarchive Berlin, Germany, Zertifikatsnummer 252.

14   Christopher Hailey, "The Call to Berlin," in *Franz Schreker (1878–1934): A Cultural Biography* (Cambridge: Cambridge University Press, 1993), p.122.

15   "It was amazing what these young Schreker students could do. We gave them contrapuntal problems to solve, examined their strict and free styles, heard one fugue after another (both vocal and instrumental), gave them themes for modulation and improvisation, examined their musicality and ear training – these students were skilled in everything. As many exams I have witnessed since, I have never again encountered such an artistic level." – from Georg Schünemann's article "Franz Schreker als Lehrer" in Franz Schreker 50th Birthday edition of *Anbruch* Magazine, March/April 1928.;

   English version: Christopher Hailey, "The Call to Berlin," in *Franz Schreker (1878–1934): A Cultural Biography* (Cambridge: Cambridge University Press, 1993), p.122.;

   Original Source: Georg Schünemann, "Franz Schreker als Lehrer," *Franz Schreker zum 50. Geburtstag* (Schreker issue), *Anbruch* 10/3-4, March/April 1928, p.109-111.

16   This concert was repeated on 26 June 1921. Source: Dietmar Schenk, Markus Böggemann, Rainer Cadenbach, *Franz Schrekers Schüler in Berlin: Biographische Beiträge und Dokumente*. Schriften aus dem UdK-Archiv Band 8 (Berlin: Universität der Künste Berlin, 2005), p.163-166.

> Herr Julius Buerger is an excellent musician – at home in opera and concert – a very good accompanist – brilliant coach for singers – and deserves every recommendation
>
> Bruno Walter

A recommendation for Julius Burger from famed conductor Bruno Walter (1876–1962) in English, circa 1924 © A-Weaz

In the same year Burger began study in conducting which only added to his impressive skill set as composer, pianist, and accompanist. After completing his studies at the Berlin Hochschule in 1922, he began work as a *korrepetitor* for Karlsruhe Opera where he would stay until 1924. It was his abilities as a conductor which later led to recognition by conductor Bruno Walter (1876–1972). Burger had apparently made a good impression on Walter after proving himself at a performance of Wagner's *Tannhäuser* with a reduced orchestra and after little rehearsal.[17] As a result, in 1924 Walter recommended that Burger be apprenticed as assistant to Arthur Bodanzsky (1877–1939) at the Metropolitan Opera in New York. Walter wrote that: *"Herr Julius Buerger is an excellent musician – at home in opera and concert – a very good accompanist, brilliant coach for singers – and deserves every recommendation."*[18]

2.2.1. Apprenticeship at the Metropolitan Opera, New York

Burger worked for three seasons with the Metropolitan Opera from 1924 to 1927 in which he served as a repetiteur, coach, and accompanist for auditions as well as the popular Met Gala Concerts which featured renowned singers such as baritone Lawrence Tibbit (1896–1960).[19] Burger also found opportunity to use his skills as a pianist through a last-minute invitation by Bodanzky to record several piano rolls for the American Piano Company's (AMPICO) line of reproducing player pianos. Burger, along with pianist Milton Suskind [*pseudonym Edgar Fairchild*] (1898–1975) and Artur Bodanzky conducting from the side, recorded four piano arrangements scored for four hands including *Parsifal and the Flower Maiden* (Wagner; Rubenstein), the overture from *Pique Dame* (von Suppè), the overture from *Sakuntala*, op. 13 (Goldmark) and Symphony No. 40 in G minor (W. A. Mozart).[20]

In 1926, while still engaged with the Metropolitan, Burger's accompanist skills were once again put into practice when he was chosen to perform with acclaimed contralto Ernestine Schumann-Heink (1861–1936) on a multi-stop tour from her home in Coronado Beach, California to San Francisco. The

---

17   Albrecht Dümling, "Melodien sind dem Emigranten näher als die Fakten der Erinnerung," *Der Tagesspiegel*, Berlin, 16 July 1994.

18   Bruno Walter, "Recommendation for Julius Bürger," Julius Burger Collection, Exilarte Zentrum Archiv der mdw, Vienna, Austria.

19   Met Opera Gala Concert – Twentieth Sunday Night Concert. Metropolitan Opera House, March 22, 1925, Metopera database, Metropolitan Opera Archives, CID: 89870, keyword search 'Julius Burger', URL: http://archives.metoperafamily.org/archives/frame.htm , Accessed 25/06/2020.

20   According to the company's 1998 catalogue, Burger's recorded titles include:
6590 (65903H): *Parsifal and the Flower Maiden* – Wagner-Rubenstein;
6494 (64943H): *Pique Dama Overture* – von Suppe – Herbert;
6533 (65333H), 6545 (65453H): *Sakuntala Overture* (2 parts) – Goldmark;
6442 (64423H), 6443 (64433H), 6449 (64493H), 6444 (64443H): *Symphony in G minor, No.40* – W. A. Mozart. Source: Albert M. Petrak (ed.), *Ampico Piano Roll Catalog*, The Reproducing Piano Roll Foundation, 1998, URL: https://www.player-care.com/ampico_catalog.pdf, accessed 23/03/2019.

tour was created to raise funds in aid of disabled veterans. This was likely to have been a convivial experience as Burger gifted Schumann-Heink a manuscript copy of his lied *Abendläuten* (1920). It now resides in the Schumann-Heink Collection at Claremont Colleges Library in California.[21]

Up to this point, Burger had completed a handful of noteworthy compositions ranging from lieder for voice and piano (*Dämmernd liegt der Sommerabend* (1915), *Seliges Ende* (1919), *Abendläuten* (1920), *Lieder im Abend* (1926)) to a pair orchestral lieder in the line of Mahler (*Legende* (1919) and *Stille Der Nacht* (1923)) as well as a choral work (*Miserere* (1917)) and a symphonic overture titled *Ozeanfahrt, 1925*. The latter was likely inspired by his annual summer voyages to Europe during the Metropolitan's off seasons.[22]

2.2.2. Return to Berlin

At the conclusion of his Metropolitan apprenticeship in 1927, Burger returned to Berlin where he gained employment in a freelance capacity with the Berlin Funkstunde as a conductor and arranger. During this period, he also served as assistant to Kroll Opera resident conductor Otto Klemperer (1885–1973). The company, formerly part of the Staatsoper Unter den Linden, was re-opened as a separate entity with an inaugural performance of Beethoven's *Fidelio* on 19 November 1927.[23] Under Klemperer, the company pursued a vision to bring opera's traditional form into the present by presenting new, progressive works which were representative of the forward thinking and experimental atmosphere of the young Weimar Republic's cultural scene. In total, 44 world premieres were presented in its short existence. These included modernist compositions by the likes of Paul Hindemith (*Neues vom Tage*, 8 June 1929) and Arnold Schoenberg (*Begleitmusik zu einer Lichtspielszene*, 6 November 1930), among other premieres of works by Ernst Krenek (*Leben des Orest*, March 1930), and Leŏs Janáček (*Z mrtvého domu*, June 1931).[24]

Unfortunately, Klemperer's attempt to modernise the operatic scene was ahead of its time and audiences didn't readily accept his vision. A conservative backlash and protests ensued. According to a late interview with Burger, conducted by Dr Trude Zörer, rumours of the company's demise had been circulating in early 1930, including that the Prussian state parliament would no longer support the Kroll Opera. Upon hearing the news, Burger offhandedly made the comment "Ich bin die erste Ratte, die dass Schiff verlässt" ("I am

---

21   Burger, Julius, "Abendläuten," *Ernestine Schumann-Heink, A Contralto's Legacy Collection*, Honnold/Mudd Library Special Collections, Claremont Colleges Digital Library, No. esh00126, URL: https://ccdl.claremont.edu/digital/collection/p15831coll6/id/688/rec/1, Accessed 18 November 2020.

22   The latter piece was later performed as part of an orchestral concert by the Berlin Radio Orchestra conducted by Bruno Seidler-Winkler and broadcast on the Berlin Funkstunde on 22 April 1931 at 8PM. Source: Playbill, "Mittwoch, den 22 April 1931 – Berlin Funkstunde," Julius Burger, '31-'42, R27/40/2, BBC Music-General, File Folder I of II, BBC Written Archives. Caversham, England.

23   Peter Heyworth, *Otto Klemperer: Volume 1, 1885–1933: His Life and Times* (Cambridge: Cambridge University Press, 1996), p.253-60.

24   Ibid, p.256.

An advert for Burger's Funkstunde/ BBC simulcast Radio Potpourri *Hallo London, Here's Berlin* (1932).
© Radio Times Magazine, 11 November 1932, Issue 476, p.441

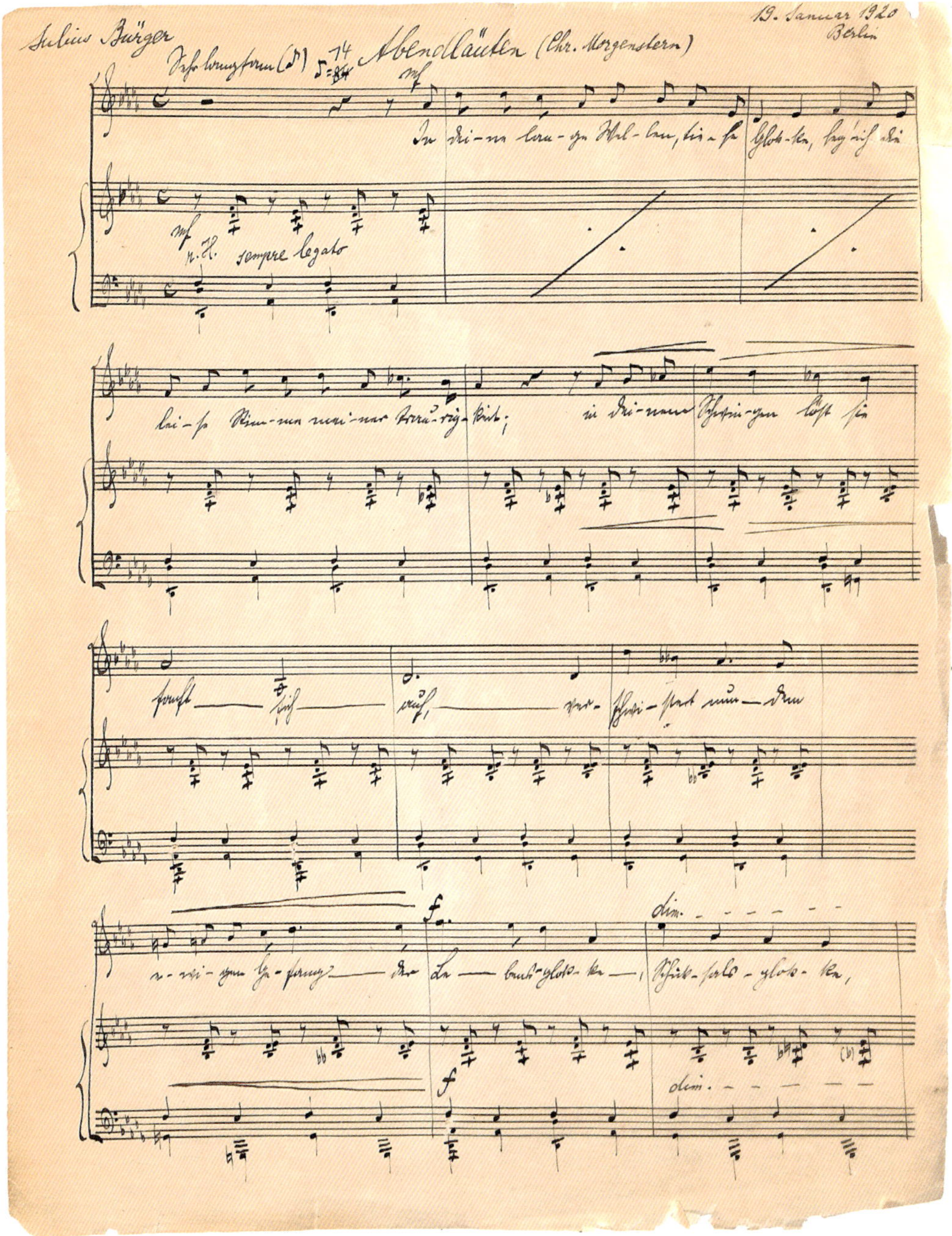

Manuscript setting of Christian Morgenstern's *Abendläuten* (1920)
© A-Weaz

the first rat to leave the ship") to a fellow member of staff. This was later relayed to Klemperer who made his displeasure known.[25] Ultimately, declining ticket sales as well as the dire economic situation in the 1930/31 season were major contributors to the company's demise. These were also main contributors to Burger's resignation with the company. He then transitioned to full time employment with the Berlin Funkstunde in 1930. This was indeed timely as the Kroll Opera closed its doors permanently at the conclusion of the 1930/31 season with a final performance of Mozart's *Le Nozze di Figaro* on 3 July 1931.[26]

The closure of the company marked a major blow to the German republic's modern cultural scene. The building itself was refashioned to house the German parliament after the Reichstag fire on 27 February 1933, where the theatre became a stage for the literal demise of Germany's Weimar Republic.

From 1930 onward, Burger was solely employed as a conductor, arranger, and composer at the relatively young Berlin Funkstunde. Here he had an early compositional success with the broadcast of his symphonic overture *Ozeanfahrt, 1925*. However, his most successful compositions with the Funkstunde, and later the BBC, were in a light entertainment genre he deemed 'Radio Potpourri'.[27] While Burger did not by any means invent the genre (composers had been creating musical potpourris since at least the eighteenth century), he is credited with remediating this traditional form for the medium of radio by expanding its length and incorporating a storyline and narration over a tapestry of musical themes. One such Radio Potpourri, titled *Hallo London, Here's Berlin* was broadcast from the Funkstunde's studios in Berlin as a simulcast in partnership with the BBC London on 14 November 1932.[28] The programme, consisting of light orchestral and vocal music from musical comedies and operas, featured tenor Joseph Schmidt (1904–1942), soprano Elisabeth Friedrich (1893–1981), soubrette Edith Schollwer (1904–2002), actor Eugene Rex (1884–1943) and was accompanied by the German Concert Orchestra, conducted by Eduard Künneke (1885–1953).[29]

This was not the first occasion Burger had worked with the Austro-Hungarian and Romanian tenor Joseph Schmidt. The two met first in the Kroll Opera and enjoyed a friendship through concert and operetta broadcasts staged for the Funkstunde. Their friendship led Burger to compose two commercial successes for Schmidt. The first, titled *Zigeunerlied* or "Gypsy Song", was recorded in February of 1930 for Ultraphon Berlin.[30] The second piece, titled *Launisches*

---

25 Julius Burger, "Julius Burger speaks to Trude Zörer on his friendship with Joseph Schmidt," interviewed by Dr. Trude Zörer, date of recording unknown, audio, 24:22, from the private collection of Dr. Trude Zörer.

26 Peter Heyworth, *Otto Klemperer: His Life and Times. Volume 1, 1885–1933* (Cambridge: Cambridge University Press, 1996) p.366-67.

27 Radio Potpourri utilise themes or sections from existing musical works which are then combined with incidental music around a central theme. They are generally self-contained and performed as a solitary piece. Scripted narration commonly accompanied the piece to supplement the performance.

28 Contributor, "Hallo London, Here's Berlin," *Radio Times,* 11 November 1932, Issue 476, p.44r.

29 Ibid.

30 Joseph Schmidt "Zigeunerlied" by Julius Bürger, Lajos Kiss and his Zigeunerorchestra, Recorded 12 February 1930, 30422, Germany: Ultraphon / Telefunken E 373, Austria: Kalliope K 702. Source: Alfred A. Fassbind, *Joseph Schmidt: Sein Lied ging um die Welt,* (Zürich: Römerhof Verlag, 2012), p.299.

Glück, utilised thematic material from Johann Strauss II's song 'O Schöner Mai' (operetta *Prinz Methusalem*) to create a new piece with lyrics by Leopold Hainisch.[31] The work was incorporated into the Strauss operetta *1,001 Nacht* which featured Schmidt and was frequently performed by the singer in concert. One such example includes the 31 October 1937 broadcast performance from New York City's Carnegie Hall.[32] *Launisches Glück* is arguably most readily recognised from the record shop scene in the 1933 German film 'Ein Lied Geht um die Welt' starring Schmidt.[33] By the time of the film's release (9 May 1933), Burger had already resigned from his position at the Funkstunde.[34] Following the Nazi Regime's seizure of power through the March 5th parliamentary elections and the subsequent passage of the Enabling Act, Burger's life in Germany became untenable. He returned to Vienna and after two previously unsuccessful relationships, married Rose (Rosa) Blaustein on 20 August 1933. They remained married for 55 years until Rose's death in 1989. Although he returned to the relative safety of the Austrian capital, the political situation in 1933 had also moved towards right wing authoritative rule under Chancellor Engelbert Dollfuß.

2.3 London period (1934–1939)

The abrupt severance from his life and burgeoning career in Berlin caused a conflict in identity for Burger as he searched for work. After several months of unemployment, he made contact with British entertainer and author Eric Maschwitz (1901–1969) who had recently been appointed the director of the BBC's newly created Variety Department. The department's programming ranged from revue, concert and music hall performances to presentations of old time musicals, radio operetta and light opera. BBC Variety's offerings were broadcast from St George's Hall, adjacent to Broadcasting

---

31 Although Burger's name is not included in Fassbind's listing, it does appear on the single which was issued in 1932 on Parlophon. Source: Joseph Schmidt, "Launisches Glück" by Julius Bürger, Leopold Hainisch, Lyrics, Staatskapelle Berlin, cond. by Dr. Weissmann, recorded 18 February 1932, 133438: Germany – B.48154, 133438-3: Germany– Parlophon B. 48154 / Odeon 0-25982, England – Parlophone R 1330, Australia – R 3550, America– Decca P-20311. Source: Alfred A. Fassbind, *Joseph Schmidt: Sein Lied ging um die Welt*, (Zürich: Römerhof Verlag, 2012), p.290.

32 Ibid, p.304.

33 Original German version: *Ein Lied geht um die Welt*, directed by Richard Oswald, (Rio Film, Premiered 9 May 1933 Ufa-Palast am Zoo, Berlin), 0:16:20 to 0:18:36. English Language adaptation: *My Song Goes Round the World*, directed by Richard Oswald, British International Pictures, 1934.

34 In response to previous correspondence with BBC Variety Department director Eric Maschwitz, Burger provided a short biography for the company to distribute to various news publications. Burger states: "Left Berlin 1933 April, on account of the Hitler Government." Source: Julius Burger, "Letter to Eric Maschwitz," 21 January 1935, From Burger, Julius. 31-42. R27/40/2. BBC Music-General: Burger, Julius. BBC Written Archives Centre, Reading, England.

A candid photo of Julius and Rose Burger in promotion of *Liebestraum* (1936). Radio Times, 31 January 1936, Vol. 50, Issue 644, p.20.

Julius and Rose ('Rosa' Blaustein) Burger. © A-Weaz

House in London.[35] The department's early success provided the impetus for the commissioning of new content.[36] Burger's previous work as a composer and arranger of similar content at the Funkstunde and his proficiency in English, developed during his apprenticeship at the Metropolitan Opera, made him a valuable contributor to the department's programme line-up. These contributions, in the form of Radio Potpourri, would go onto shape and influence BBC Variety programming into the 1950s.

Burger's first commissioned work for the corporation was the Radio Potpourri *Vienna* (1933). (A previous potpourri, *Hallo London, Here's Berlin* (1932), was given a simultaneous broadcast on BBC and Funkstunde radio frequencies two years previously. However, Burger was uncredited for this work.) *Vienna*, broadcast on the BBC London regional programme on 4 January 1934 followed by a repeat broadcast on the national programme the following evening, was an hour-long arrangement utilising music by Johann Strauss II (1825–1899) and Joseph Lanner (1801–1843). The broadcast also marked Burger's conducting debut in the UK.[37] Although one review in the *Birmingham Gazette* was unfavorable, the work was considered a success by those in the Variety Department.[38] Shortly thereafter, Maschwitz commissioned two further Radio Potpourri programmes from Burger and his collaborator – Viennese author, Artur Kulka.[39] Titles included a musical tour of Europe in *Holiday in Europe* (1934)[40] as well as a biographic recollection of Jacques Offenbach in the Radio Potpourri, *Life of Offenbach* (1934).[41] The plasticity of the genre, coupled with Burger's aptitude for innovative thematic concepts, led to seven more Grand

---

35 Martin Dibbs, "1933–1939: the Show Begins" from *Radio Fun and the BBC Variety Dept., 1922-67: Comedy and Popular Music on Air* (Cham: Palgrave Macmillian, 2019), p.48-49.

36 Ibid., p.51-55.

37 *Vienna* premiered on 4 January 1934 on the BBC London Regional Service at 9:15PM. Source: Contributor, "Vienna," *Radio Times*, 29 December 1933, Vol.41, Issue 535, p.972, 976.

38 Contributor, "Not So Dreamy Vienna," *Brimingham Gazette*, 4 January 1934, No. 27,996, p.6.

39 Artur Kulka is credited with writing the narration for two of Burger's early radio potpourri for the BBC including *Vienna* (1933) and *Holiday in Europe* (1934). Kulka was also forced into exile after the Austrian annexation by Nazi Germany on 13 March 1938. His name is among the Jewish members blacklisted by Austria's society of authors, composers, and music publishers (*Staatlich genehmigte Gesellschaft der Autoren, Komponisten und Musikverlager*). An annotated copy of the organisation's 1937 directory, noting those with Jewish ancestry, was discovered in the Vienna City Library in 2010 by Dr. Christoph Lind.

The citation provided includes a digitized copy of the document with Kulka's name appearing on page 13. Source: Carla Sapreau, "The Austrian Copyright Society and Blacklisting During the Nazi Era," OREL Foundation, August 2014, Accessed 18 January 2022, URL: http://orelfoundation.org/journal/journalArticle/the_austrian_copyright_society_and_blacklisting_during_the_nazi_era#07302014_1

40 *Holiday in Europe* premiered 17 July 1934 on BBC London Regional Service at 9:15PM. Source: Contributor, "Holiday in Europe," *Radio Times*, Vol. 44, Issue 563, p.105, 112.

41 *Life of Offenbach* premiered 7 January 1935 on BBC National Service at 9PM.
Source: Contributor, "Life of Offenbach," *Radio Times*, 4 January 1935, Vol.46, Issue 588, p.7, 28, 31.

Burger performs a tune on the piano after rehearsals for the May 1936 broadcast premiere of *Festival of Folk Music*. BBC Studios – London.
© Radio Times, 1 May 1936, Vol. 51, Issue 657, p.20.

Photo from the 1931 production of *1,001 Nacht* – starring tenor Joseph Schmidt in the lead role. The production was broadcast by the Berlin Funkstunde and featured Burger's Strauss inspired lied 'Launisches Glück'. © Joseph Schmidt Archiv, Zürich

potpourris, a serialised 'Chapter potpourri,' as well as dozens of shorter arrangements being produced over the following five years.[42]

The BBC commissions served as a financial lifeline for the composer but the political turmoil in Germany and Austria presented further issues for the young composer. While other émigrés at the BBC, such as Walter Goehr, Mátyás Seiber, Leo Wurmser, Ernst Hermann Meyer, Artur Willner, Franz Reizenstein, and Berthold Goldschmidt, had found security in full-time employment at the Corporation, Burger's engagement with the BBC as a 'per contract' composer precluded him from gaining a visa.[43] This became an increasingly pressing issue as the Nazi regime exerted more influence in Europe. The threat was recognised as early as January 1934 by one British radio listener who penned an op-ed to the *Leeds Mercury* newspaper regarding Burger, titled "Should He Be Turned Away?"[44] Since leaving Berlin in 1933, Julius and Rose lived an increasingly transient existence. The couple stayed for shorter and shorter lengths of time in Vienna and with greater frequency between London and Brussels.[45] An October 1936 petition to the UK Ministry of Labour as well as a subsequent appeal to the Home Office proved unsuccessful.[46] From September 1937, the Burgers resided in Paris, only returning to London for the first few weeks of 1938.

While his legal status was a constant struggle, Burger was successful in Britain in other respects. Unlike the relatively few works by fellow émigrés which were successfully broadcast by the BBC between 1933 and 1945, Burger had at least thirteen Grand potpourris as well as multiple Miniature potpourris, arrangements and orchestrations premiered during this period. The majority of these were also rebroadcast or revived. Even during the Second World War, at least six of his Radio Potpourris were included in programming, with several being broadcast more than once. These included *The Empire Sings!* (18 February 1940), *Johann Strauss: A Biography in Music* (19 July 1942, 14 May 1944, 6 August 1944), *Liebestraum* (7 March 1943, 24 September 1944, 25 March 1945), *New World Rhapsody* (3 and 5 March 1944, 20

---

42 See the Radio Potpourri section for a comprehensive list and more details about specific titles.

43 Florian Scheding, 'Problematic Tendencies': Émigré Composers in London, 1933–1945" from *The Impact of Nazism on Twentieth-Century Music*. (ed.) Erik Levi. (Vienna: Böhlau Verlag, 2014) p. 247-271.

44 The brief contribution highlights the anti-Semitic discrimination Burger faced in Germany while focusing on the composer's success and skill as a musician. The contributor then chastised the UK Home Office's policy severely limiting the admission of foreign musicians and draws comparisons between Burger and Friedrich Händel to emphasise the important contributions immigrants can add to British culture. Source: Op-ed, "Should He Be Turned Away?" *The Leeds Mercury*, 6 January 1934, Issue No.29,376, p.6.

45 In correspondence with Eric Maschwitz, Burger expresses his intent to leave Vienna for a new life in Brussels on 28 February 1935. Subsequent letters throughout 1935 in the BBC Written Archive's collection show correspondence addresses in Brussels and England.
Source: Julius Burger, "Letter to Eric Maschwitz," 12 February 1935, From Burger, Julius. 31-42. R27/40/2. BBC Music-General: Burger, Julius. BBC Written Archives Centre, Reading, England.

46 Mark Lubbock, "Dr. Julius Burger," BBC Internal Memo, 28 October 1936, From Burger, Julius. 31-42. R27/40/2. BBC Music-General: Burger, Julius. BBC Written Archives Centre, Reading, England. Letter from Home Office, Whitehall to BBC Variety Department, RE: Julius Burger, 10 November 1936, Ref. no. B.7058, From Burger, Julius. 31-42. R27/40/2. BBC Music-General: Burger, Julius. BBC Written Archives Centre, Reading, England.

August 1944), *City of Music* (9 July 1944), and *Life of Offenbach* (3 September 1944, 5 November 1944).

In early February 1938, the Burgers had made plans to travel back to Austria for the first time in several months in anticipation of a possible plebiscite vote on the question of Austria's absorption into the German Reich. According to Burger, the couple were at a scheduled stopover in France when he noticed a newspaper headline exclaiming "Austrian Chancellor meets Hitler." The couple immediately fled the train and abandoned their plans to return to Vienna.[47] They instead proceeded to the French Riviera where they resided at the Hotel Belles Rives in the resort town of Antibes.[48] After news had reached the couple of Austria's annexation by Germany on 12 March 1938, the Burger's returned to Paris. Throughout these life-altering weeks, Burger apparently took solace in composition and completed his ode to the British Empire, aptly titled *The Empire Sings!* (5 April 1938).[49] The Burgers would not return to Vienna for many years after the 2ⁿᵈ World War's conclusion.

According to internal documents and correspondence now housed in the BBC Written Archives, the Burgers returned to London in May for the premiere of *The Empire Sings!* (1938). After a final application to stay in the UK proved unsuccessful, the Burgers were granted a limited extension to remain in the UK while gathering supporting material for an asylum application to the United States. In a letter to colleague Stanford Robinson in July of that year, Burger wrote *"[o]ur sky is quite dark for the moment, but we do not lose courage."*[50]

Fortunately, Burger gained letters of support from the BBC's staff and administration, including P. E. Cruttwell, the programme contracts executive.[51] After an arduous search through a large list of international contacts, his application

---

47 Dr. Trude Zörer, "Interview by Ryan Hugh Ross on the life of Julius Burger (Bürger)," Question No.25, 30 October 2019.

48 Two letters of correspondence from this period notes the address as Hotel Belles Rives with the next letter, dated 14 April 1938, addressed from the Hotel de Normandie in Paris.

Sources: Julius Burger, "Letter to Stanford Robinson," 4 March 1938, From Burger, Julius. 31-42. R27/40/2. BBC Music-General: Burger, Julius. BBC Written Archives Centre, Reading, England.

Stanford Robinson, "Letter to Julius Burger," 10 March 1938, From Burger, Julius. 31-42. R27/40/2. BBC Music-General: Burger, Julius. BBC Written Archives Centre, Reading, England.

Julius Burger, "Letter to Stanford Robinson," 14 April 1938, From Burger, Julius. 31-42. R27/40/2. BBC Music-General: Burger, Julius. BBC Written Archives Centre, Reading, England.

49 Also known under the title "Songs of the British Empire", this work utilises traditional native music as well as colonial folk songs from British dominions and colonies from across the world to provide a musical survey of the empire as it existed in 1938.

Source: Julius Burger, *The Empire Sings!*, (unpublished manuscript score, 4 April 1938), BBC No. MSS6401 – Buerger. EaZ-035-03-00021. Box 3, No. 1.3.7. Julius Burger (Bürger) Collection. Exilarte Zentrum Archiv der mdw. Vienna, Austria. p.283.

50 Julius Burger, "Letter to Stanford Robinson," 18 July 1938, From Burger, Julius. 31-42. R27/40/2. BBC Music-General: Burger, Julius. BBC Written Archives Centre, Reading, England.

51 P.E. Cruttwell, "Letter of support to American Embassy in London for Julius Burger," 19 July 1938, From Burger, Julius. 31-42. R27/40/2. BBC Music-General: Burger, Julius. BBC Written Archives Centre, Reading, England.

Should He Be Turned Away?

LISTENERS to the broadcast programmes—and most of us are listeners these days—have been charmed by the delightful pot-pourri "Vienna," produced by Julius Bürger, and will be interested in what is to happen to this man.

He has obtained fame on the Continent for his production of radio pot-pourris, a field of activity he has made his own, but has been driven from Germany owing to his Jewish blood. The B.B.C. invited him to this country to produce his arrangement of "Vienna." Now, despite the dictum that art should know no national boundaries, the Home Office will not let him remain here for more than a week.

The justification claimed by the Home Office for this action is that we have many musicians out of work. Its policy would have excluded from our shores many master musicians, such as Handel, who have added to our glories.

If it is to our advantage to give a home to precious books, is it not also advantageous to give a home to artists who are masters? Is there not a need of such a man as Julius Bürger to aid our great broadcast organisation?

Op-ed article from January 1934 which highlights Julius Burger's situation as an exile. From the Leeds Mercury Newspaper. 6 January 1934. No. 29, 367. P.6.

Burger poses on the conductor's podium (BBC Studios – London) in this promo photo for the 1935 premiere of *World Tour*. © Radio Times, 22 Nov. 1935, Vol.49, Issue 634, p.76.

JULIUS BUERGER, whose new pot-pourri, 'World Tour', produced and conducted by Stanford Robinson, will be presented this evening at 7.0.

was completed with an affidavit of support from American tenor Charles Kullman (1903–1983) whom he had previously worked with in Europe.[52] Burger continued to be actively involved with the BBC over the remaining months of 1938, composing and arranging for the series *Songs of the British Isles*. The serial featured arrangements of well-known traditional folk tunes from across the home territories. Several examples of his contributions include three miniature pot-pourri works on various themes including *Morris Dances*,[53] *Regimental Marches*[54] and *Sea Shanties*.[55]

After a successful application to the US Embassy, the Burgers left England for New York from Southampton aboard the RMS Aquitania on 25 March 1939. They arrived in New York City six days later. Poignantly, their nationality is listed as "Stateless".[56] Back in Europe, Burger's name later joined the hundreds of artists and musicians, who were effectively blacklisted, in the notorious Nazi sponsored encyclopaedia *Lexikon der Juden in der Musik* (1940).[57]

Burger had composed and arranged an impressively large collection of musical creations for the BBC and, along with the two commercial hits written for Joseph Schmidt, had continued to compose noteworthy works of a serious nature after 1927. These include a symphonic suite titled the *Eastern*

---

52 Julius Burger, "Julius Burger speaks to Trude Zörer on his friendship with Joseph Schmidt," interviewed by Dr. Trude Zörer, date of recording unknown, audio, 24:22, from the Private collection of Dr. Trude Zörer.

53 "Morris Dances" was included in the third installment of the programme "Songs of the British Isles" and was first broadcast on 14 August 1938 on the BBC National Service at 9:05PM.

Source: Contributor, "Songs of the British Isles, No.3," *Radio Times*, 12 August 1938, Vol. 60, Issue 776, p.13, 27.

54 "Regimental Marches" was included in the fourth installment of "Songs of the British Isles" and was first broadcast 18 September 1938 on the BBC National Service at 9:05PM. The work includes standard marching tunes associated with selected regiments of the British military including *The Lincolnshire Poacher* , *Speed the Plough* , *Wi' a Hundred Pipers*, *The British Grenadiers*, *Men of Harlech*, *John Peel* and *Life on the Ocean Wave*. Sources: Contributor, "Songs of the British Isles No.4," *Radio Times*, 16 September 1938, Vol.60, Issue 781, p.22.

BBC Internal Memo, "Julius Burger's Miniature Pot-pourri of Military Marches for 'Songs of the British Isles' ", 18 September 1938, From Burger, Julius. 31-42. R27/40/2. BBC Music-General: Burger, Julius. BBC Written Archives Centre, Reading, England.

55 "Sea Shanties" was included in the sixth installment of "Songs of the British Isles" and was first broadcast on the BBC Regional Service on 7 November 1938 at 8:30PM.

Source: Contributor, "Songs of the British Isles, No.6," *Radio Times*, 4 November 1938, Vol. 61, Issue 788, p.34.

56 Passenger Lists of Vessels Arriving at New York, New York, 1820–1897. Microfilm Publication M237, 675 rolls. NAI: 6256867. Records of the U.S. Customs Service, Record Group 36. National Archives at Washington, D.C. ;

Passenger Lists of Vessels Arriving at New York, New York, 1820–1897. Microfilm Publication M237, 675 rolls. NAI: 6256867. Records of the U.S. Customs Service, Record Group 36. National Archives at Washington, D.C.

57 Theo Stengel, Herbert Gerigk, *Lexikon der Juden in der Musik*, (Berlin: Bernhard Ahnefeld Verlag, 1940), p.44.

Burger composing in the summer of 1939. Connecticut, USA. © A-Weaz

Symphony (1931–35),[58] *Concerto for Cello and Orchestra* (1932),[59] *Variations on a Theme by Carl Phillip Emanuel Bach* (1933; completed 1945),[60] and the *Symphonic Scherzo for Strings* (1937).[61] Several unsuccessful attempts were made to get various selections of these works broadcast by the BBC including his *Concerto for Cello and Orchestra* (1932),[62] an arrangement of *Zigeunerlied* for violin and orchestra and the "Oriental Suite," also known as the *Eastern Symphony*.[63] To date, Burger's *Suite of 5 Little Pieces from Vienna*, broadcast on the BBC National Service on 14 December 1937, is his only non-commissioned work successfully broadcast by the corporation until his 1939 departure.[64]

---

58   This work was previously titled *Near and Far*. It was started in 1931 Berlin and completed in 1935 according to archival documentation. Sources: Julius Burger, "Personal notebook on compositions," Private collections of Dr. Trude Zörer, Vienna, Austria, p.42. ;
Lynne S. Mazza, "Eastern Symphony", Program notes for The Orchestra of St. Luke's, *The Music of Julius Burger*, Paul Lustig Dunkel, conductor, 3 June 1991, Alice Tully Hall – Lincoln Center, New York, NY, p.13-16A.

59   Julius Burger, Personal notebook on compositions, Private collections of Dr. Trude Zörer, Vienna, Austria, p.44. ; Lynne S. Mazza, "Concerto for Cello and Orchestra", Program notes for The Orchestra of St. Luke's, The Music of Julius Burger, Paul Lustig Dunkel, conductor, Maya Beiser, cello, 3 June 1991, Alice Tully Hall, Lincoln Center, New York, NY, p.13-16A.

60   This work was begun in 1933 Berlin but was not completed until 1945 in New York City.
Sources: Julius Burger, Personal notebook on compositions, Private collections of Dr. Trude Zörer, Vienna, Austria, p.42. ; Lynne S. Mazza, "Variations on a Theme by Carl Phillipp Emanuel Bach", Program notes for The Orchestra of St. Luke's, *The Music of Julius Burger*, Paul Lustig Dunkel, conductor, 3 June 1991, Alice Tully Hall, Lincoln Center, New York, NY, p.13-16A. ; Malcolm MacDonald, "Julius Burger (1897–1995): Orchestral Music," Liner Notes, Radio Symphonie Orchester, Berlin, cond. Simone Young, recorded 26-28, 30 September 1994, Toccata Classics, TOCC 0001, 2007, CD, p.9.

61   Listed as composed in 1937: Source: Lynne S. Mazza, "Variations on a Theme by Carl Phillipp Emanuel Bach", Program notes for The Orchestra of St. Luke's, *The Music of Julius Burger*, Paul Lustig Dunkel, conductor, 3 June 1991, Alice Tully Hall, Lincoln Center, New York, NY, p.13-16A. ;
Listed as composed in 1939: Source: Malcolm MacDonald, "Julius Burger (1897–1995): Orchestral Music," Liner Notes, Radio Symphonie Orchester, Berlin, cond. Simone Young, recorded 26-28, 30 September 1994, Toccata Classics, TOCC 0001, 2007, CD, p.8.

62   Julius Burger, "Rejection Letter from BBC to Julius Burger re: Concerto for Cello and Orchestra," 27 July 1936, From Burger, Julius. 31-42. R27/40/2. BBC Music-General: Burger, Julius. BBC Written Archives Centre, Reading, England.

63   Julius Burger, "Letter to Stanford Robinson-BBC, 18 September 1934," From Burger, Julius. 31-42. R27/40/2. BBC Music-General: Burger, Julius. BBC Written Archives Centre, Reading, England ;
Julius Burger, "Rejection Letter from Stanford Robinson to Julius Burger," 21 December 1934, From Burger, Julius. 31-42. R27/40/2. BBC Music-General: Burger, Julius. BBC Written Archives Centre, Reading, England.

64   *Suite of 5 Little Pieces from Vienna* was broadcast 14 December 1937 at 10:20PM on BBC National Service, BBC Theatre Orchestra, Leader Tate Gilder, Conducted by Stanford Robinson.
Source: Contributor, "Suite of Five Little Pieces from Vienna," *Radio Times*, 10 December 1937, Vol. 57, Issue 741, p. 44.

The Nazi endorsed *Lexicon of Jews in Music* which acted as a 'ban book' for Jewish artists and musicians in the wider Reich. Julius Burger's name is listed toward the top of 2nd column on p.44.

Theo Stengel, Herbert Gerigk, *Lexikon der Juden in der Musik* (Berlin: Bernhard Ahnefeld Verlag, 1940), p.44

2.4 New York period (1939–1995)

Over a decade after he last set foot in New York City, Julius Burger returned in drastically different circumstances. Despite possessing good command of English and several leads from his colleagues at the BBC, he had few job prospects. The Burgers settled into an apartment in Queens and shortly thereafter, Julius found employment as a freelance arranger with Columbia Broadcasting System (CBS) in early 1940. His primary work during this period was arranging for classical middlebrow stalwarts Andre Kostelanetz (1901–1980) and Arthur Fiedler (1894–1979).[65] While grateful for the employment, Burger lamented the difference between the BBC's treatment of composers to that of CBS in an April 1941 letter to BBC conductor Stanford Robinson, writing: *"But my work here cannot be compared with the one I did in England. Please, I was an artist after all. This country levels you down to a pattern. But I think I must not complain."*[66]

A short glance at the vast Kostelanetz catalogue reveals dozens of arrangements by Burger including one original work titled *Roumanian Fantasy* (1942). This was later recorded by the conductor and released in November 1944 on the Columbia Masterworks label.[67] The work appears to draw inspiration from composer George Enescu's *Romanian Rhapsodies No. 1 and 2* (1901–2). Although Burger is not credited as the originator of *Roumanian Fantasy* on the Columbia recording, the original sketch for the work as well as supplemental documentation located among his collection in Exilarte Archiv confirms the authenticity of his authorship.[68]

Throughout the war years, Burger set upon the momentous task of aiding his immediate family financially while attempting to garner the necessary visa documentation for their safe passage to the US. He found success on behalf of his brother Bernhard Bürger while two other siblings, Stefanie, and Max, emigrated to England and Palestine respectively. Burger was also successful in procuring an affidavit and financial support for his mother in Vienna which were then forwarded to her residence. However, these materials never arrived and shortly after, contact ceased.[69] Burger did not learn the fate of his remaining family until the war's conclusion. Four brothers

---

65 Julius Burger, "Letter to Stanford Robinson," 6 August 1940, From Burger, Julius. 31-42. R27/40/2. BBC Music-General: Burger, Julius. BBC Written Archives Centre, Reading, England.

66 Julius Burger, "Letter to Stanford Robinson," 15 April 1941, From Burger, Julius. 31-42. R27/40/2. BBC Music-General: Burger, Julius. BBC Written Archives Centre, Reading, England.

67 Andre Kostelanetz and his Orchestra, "Roumanian Fantasy," 1946, Columbia Masterworks 7427-M, XCO 33901, 78rpm.

68 Julius Burger, "Letter to Stanford Robinson," 22 February 1945, From Burger, Julius. 31-42. R27/40/2. BBC Music-General: Burger, Julius. BBC Written Archives Centre, Reading, England ;

Julius Burger, "Letter to Stanford Robinson," 5 October 1945, From Burger, Julius. 31-42. R27/40/2. BBC Music-General: Burger, Julius. BBC Written Archives Centre, Reading, England ;

Julius Burger, "Letter to Stanford Robinson," 23 November 1945, From Burger, Julius. 31-42. R27/40/2. BBC Music-General: Burger, Julius. BBC Written Archives Centre, Reading, England.

69 Dr. Trude Zörer, "Interview by Ryan Hugh Ross on the life of Julius Burger (Bürger)," Question No.31, 30 October 2019.

and his mother, Chaje, were murdered in the Holocaust.[70] A fifth brother's fate still remains unknown. This tragic blow later prompted Burger to dedicate the second *Adagio* movement of his *Concerto for Cello and Orchestra*, to his mother's memory.[71]

After years of uncertainty, the Burgers had secured financial stability and permanent residence in New York City. The couple became US citizens on 23 May 1944.[72] In line with many émigrés of the period, they chose to anglicise the spelling of their surname and dropped the Germanic umlaut.

Over the next several years, Burger continued arranging for CBS while simultaneously fulfilling further Radio Potpourri commissions for the BBC. These included an 'American' work – *New World Rhapsody* (1942) – and the *Victory Rhapsody* (1945). The latter was premiered on 13 May 1945 on

---

70 The Documentation Archive of the Austrian Resistance lists brothers Solomon, Elias and Siegfried as having been deported to the concentration / death camp complex of Auschwitz-Birkenau, Poland. His elder brother Isaak was deported on 20 October 1939 to on the Nisko relocation transports from Vienna and was not seen again. According to a 15 April 1941 letter to Stanford Robinson, Burger states his brother Elias was living in Nice, France and had obtained a visa to enter the US. Unfortunately, this did not occur and he was deported to Auschwitz-Birkenau on 4 September 1942. Sources: Victims search, Stiftung Dokumentationsarchiv des österreichischen Widerstandes (DÖW), Vienna, Austria. surname search 'Bürger', https://www.doew.at/impressum, Accessed 14 November 2021.;

Julius Burger, "Letter to Stanford Robinson," 15 April 1941, From Burger, Julius. 31-42. R27/40/2. BBC Music-General: Burger, Julius. BBC Written Archives Centre, Reading, England.

71 After many inquiries, it was made evident Burger's mother, Chaje or 'Clara', was deported from Vienna to Theresienstadt Concentration Camp and was later shot in transit. A further document in the Burger collection states Chaje and brother Siegfried were deported to Theresienstadt on 9 October 1942 and, as of 16 January 1946, had not returned to Vienna.

Equally, Burger's dedication to the second *Adagio* movement of his *Concerto for Cello and Orchestra* provides further information about his mother. On the top margin, he lists his mother's death aged 78 years on 28 September 1942.

While it is certain Mrs. Bürger was deported and perished in the late months of 1942, other sources provide conflicting information. The Documentation Archive of the Austrian Resistance (Stiftung Dokumentationsarchiv des österreichischen Widerstandes) lists her deportation date as 20 August 1942 and her death on 21 November 1942. The latter alternative date is supported by the Jewish Committee for Theresienstadt in Vienna's 1971 Austrian publication *Totenbuch Theresienstadt: Deportierte aus Österreich* which also lists Mrs. Bürger's death as 21 November 1942.

An interview conducted in 2019 with family friend, Dr. Trude Zörer, confirms while initial information led Burger to believe his mother died from her gunshot wound, she did enter the camp at Theresienstadt where she remained for approximately three months before further deportation and execution at Auschwitz-Birkenau death camp.

Sources: Victims search, Stiftung Dokumentationsarchiv des österreichischen Widerstandes (DÖW), Vienna, Austria. surname search 'Chaje Bürger', https://www.doew.at/impressum, Accessed 14 November 2021.; Bürger, Klara, listed in *Totenbuch Theresienstadt I: Deportierte aus Österreich* (Vienna: Jüdisches Komitee für Theresienstadt Wien, 1971) p.17. ;

Dr. Trude Zörer, "Interview by Ryan Hugh Ross on the life of Julius Burger (Bürger)," Question No.31, 30 October 2019.

72 Julius Burger, U.S. Certificate of Naturalization, No.6230511, Petition No.407406, from Julius Burger Collection, Exilarte Archiv der mdw, Vienna, Austria.

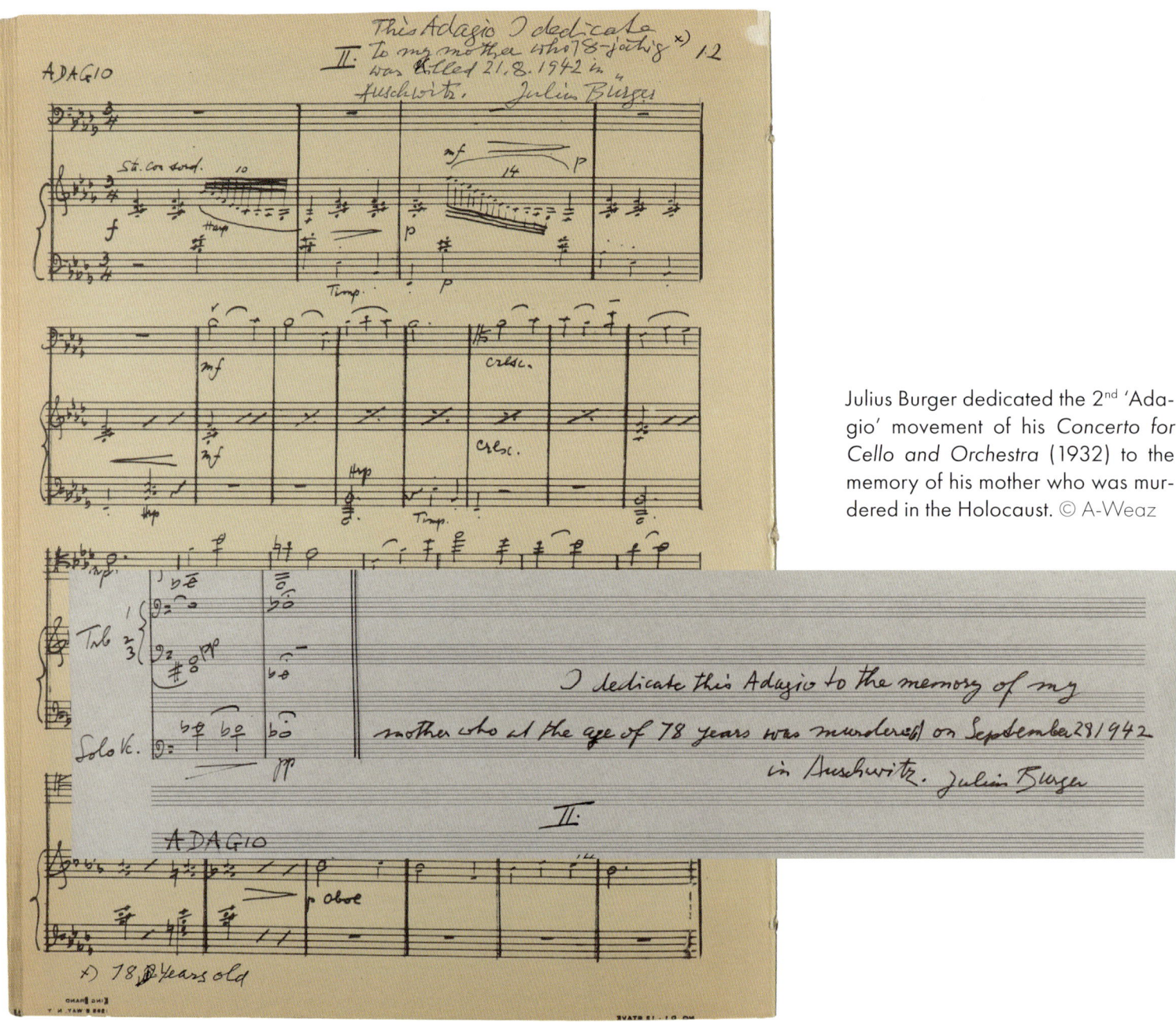

Julius Burger dedicated the 2nd 'Adagio' movement of his *Concerto for Cello and Orchestra* (1932) to the memory of his mother who was murdered in the Holocaust. © A-Weaz

Julius Burger posing at the piano. Date unknown. © A-Weaz

the BBC Home Service as part of its Victory in Europe celebrations.[73] In addition to the copious amount of composition and arranging, Burger also performed in the orchestra of the Metropolitan Opera in the 1944–45 season while accepting conducting engagements.[74]

In November 1944, Burger made his debut on Broadway as conductor for the operetta *Song of Norway*.[75] The fictional story, adapted by Robert Wright (1914–2005) and George Forrest (1915–1999) from the book by Homer Curran (1885–1952) and Milton Lazarus (1899–1955), centres on the young composer Edvard Grieg as he strives to create an authentic national sound for Norway. The music score utilised adapted musical selections from Grieg's œuvre.[76] The original production also featured traditional Norwegian folk dances and ballet, choreographed by George Balanchine (1904–1983). While the work enjoyed success in the United States and later in London, Burger's involvement was limited to New York and concluded in the autumn of 1945.[77]

In 1946, Burger was again engaged as a conductor. In this instance, he worked on the music album version of the Universal Pictures film *Song of Scheherazade* which featured friend, tenor Charles Kullman.[78] The album, released on Columbia Masterworks, features repertoire by Nikolai Rimsky-Korsakov (1844–1908) including selections from his popular opera repertoire ("Song of India" from *Sadko*, "Hymn to the Sun" from *Le Coq d'Or*) as well as an adaptation of his "Fandan-

---

[73] *Victory Rhapsody* (1945), also known as *The Nations Sing!* was broadcast five times throughout 1945 with three performances in May (13th, 17th, and 20th) and two in November (18th and 20th) of that year.

Sources: Contributor, *Victory Rhapsody*, Radio Times, 11 May 1945, Vol. 87, No.1128, p.10, 12, 21. ; Contributor, *The Nations Sing!*, Radio Times, 16 November 1945, Vol. 89, Issue 1155, p.10, 15.

[74] It is unknown the extent of Burger's involvement in performing with the Metropolitan opera's orchestra. However, he mentions playing in their productions of Richard Strauss' *Der Rosenkavalier*, *Tosca* and *Il Tabarro* in a letter to Stanford Robinson dated 22 February 1945.

Source: Julius Burger, "Letter to Stanford Robinson," 22 February 1945, From Burger, Julius. '42 - '51. R27/40/2. BBC Music-General: Burger, Julius. BBC Written Archives Centre, Reading, England.

[75] Julius Burger, "Letter to Stanford Robinson," 11 January 1945, From Burger, Julius. '42 - '51. R27/40/2. BBC Music-General: Burger, Julius. BBC Written Archives Centre, Reading, England.

[76] The operetta was adapted by Robert Wright and George Forest and was premiered at Imperial Theatre, NYC on 21 August 1944.

Source: The Broadway League, "Song of Norway," Internet Broadway Database (IBDB), 2001-02, URL: https://www.ibdb.com/broadway-production/song-of-norway-1320#People, Accessed 15 January 2022.

[77] These two letters give a rough outline of Burger's involvement as conductor of *Song of Norway*. The first letter notes he commenced on the engagement in November of 1944 while the latter, from 5 October 1945, notes he left the show to focus on orchestrating.

Sources: Julius Burger, "Letter to Stanford Robinson," 11 January 1945, From Burger, Julius. 31-42. R27/40/2. BBC Music-General: Burger, Julius. BBC Written Archives Centre, Reading, England ; Julius Burger, "Letter to Stanford Robinson," 5 October 1945, From Burger, Julius. 31-42. R27/40/2. BBC Music-General: Burger, Julius. BBC Written Archives Centre, Reading, England.

[78] Charles Kullman, *Song of Scheherazade: Music by Rimsky-Korsokov form the Universal Picture*, cond. Julius Burger, recorded 1946, Columbia Masterworks set X-272, 1946, Shellac 78rpm.

go" from the *Capriccio Espagnol*. The album is completed with the inclusion of the "Gypsy Song", adapted from two separate themes in the second version of the symphony *Antar*.[79] The film, directed by Walter Reisch (1903–1983), was released the following year and conveys a fictitious story around the composer Nicolai Rimsky-Korsakov as a young Russian naval officer (played by French actor Jean-Pierre Aumont (1911–2001)) on leave in Morocco in 1865. Its release marked Kullman's first major screen appearance in the United States as the Russian ship's doctor, Dr Klin.[80]

In 1949, Burger returned to the staff of the Metropolitan Opera as an assistant conductor.[81] This not only provided more financial stability and an opportunity to once again work in theatre, but equally surrounded Burger with a collegiate staff largely comprised of émigrés. Among recognisable names are the Metropolitan's general manager Rudolf Bing (1902–1997), chorus master Kurt Adler (1907–1977), assistant chorus master Walter Taussig (1908–2003), assistant conductors Tibor Kozma (1909–1976), Renato Cellini (1912–1976), Pietro Cimara (1887–1967) and former Schreker student Martin Rich (1905–2000).

Burger's primary responsibilities as an assistant conductor ranged from accompanying at the company's Gala events and the annual Metropolitan Opera competition to aiding in performances from the prompt box. He also served as a repetiteur and coach to the contracted singers.[82] Several examples of singers with which Burger associated with include the African American contralto Marian Anderson (1897–1993) whom he coached for her 1955 debut as Ulrica in Verdi's *Un ballo in maschera*[83] as well as the Spanish soprano Victoria de Los Angeles (1923–2005). Burger coached the latter for her role as Marguerite in the Peter Brook (1925–2022) production Gounod's *Faust*.[84] Burger also enjoyed a collegial friendship with American Bass Jerome Hines (1921–2003), made ap-

---

79 John Ball, Jr., "Song of Scheherazade," liner notes for Charles Kullman, *Song of Scheherazade: Music by Rimsky-Korsokov form the Universal Picture*, cond. Julius Burger, recorded 1946, Columbia Masterworks set X-272, 1946, Shellac 78rpm.

80 *"Song of Scheherazade,"* Internet Movie Database (IMDb), Accessed 05 January 2022, URL: https://www.imdb.com/title/tt0039852/.

81 "New Metropolitan Aides: Burger, Taussig, De Angelis and Vivante Assistant Conductors," *The New York Times*, Col.XCIX, No.33,523, 5 November 1949, p.10.

82 Chapter fifteen of Rudolf Bing's published memoirs *5000 Nights at the Opera* includes a photograph of Burger in his prompting duties featured along with general manager Rudolf Bing, soprano Eleanor Steber, composers Samuel Barber and Gian Carlo Menotti as well as stage director Nathaniel Merrill. Source: Rudolf Bing, *5000 Nights at the Opera*, photo insert no.24. (New York: Doubleday and Company, Inc., 1972), p.144-145.

83 Anderson was the first African American to perform a major role at the Metropolitan Opera on 7 January 1955. Sources: Howard Taubman, "Marian Anderson Wins Ovation In First Opera Role at the 'Met'," *The New York Times*, 8 January 1955, p.1, 11. ; Michael Ryan, "The Concert of a Lifetime," *Parade Magazine*, 5 September 1993, p.40-41.

84 Howard Taubman, "The Remaking of an Opera: How the Met's 'Faust' was divested of familiar medieval trappings and made to look this season the way its romantic 19th century music sounds." *The New York Times*, 22 November 1953, p.120, 255, 269, 271, 272.

parent in comedic concert antics as part of the Met's post-performance receptions.⁸⁵ Further evidence of their friendship is highlighted by the recently discovered copy of Burger's 1919 orchestral lied *Legende* in the Hines collection at Howard Gottlieb Archival Research Center at Boston University. The manuscript copy has been transposed for bass voice.⁸⁶

While Burger's knowledge of the operatic voice and repertoire coupled with his experience in the field made him a valued coach at the Metropolitan, evidence suggests he had not entirely given up on his compositional career and continued to promote his original works. One such performance includes the premiere of his *Concerto for Cello and Orchestra* (in reduced arrangement for cello and two pianos) which was held as part of a recital in New York Town Hall on 2 October 1952. The work, performed by Latvian cellist Ingus Naruns (1925–2012) accompanied by Burger and Antolijis Berzkalns (?), received a warm reception but would not be performed in any further capacity until 1991.⁸⁷

In 1954, Burger's skills in composition and arrangement were once again put to use; this time by the Metropolitan Opera.

Since his appointment as general manager, Rudolf Bing had made many changes in an attempt to revitalise the company and in mid-1954, Bing commissioned ballet master Zachary Solov (1923–2004) and Burger to create a one-act ballet. The result was *Vittorio*, a forty-five-minute work in three scenes. It premiered on 15 December 1954 in a double bill with a production of Richard Strauss' *Salome*.⁸⁸ *Vittorio* represented the Metropolitan's first commissioned ballet since the 1930s.⁸⁹ It utilised a storyline devised and choreographed by Zachary Solov. The score, devised by Burger, was arranged and orchestrated utilising thematic fragments from Verdi operas (including portions of *Un Giorno di Regno* with additional material from *Don Carlo, I Lombardi, Araido, Alzire, Giovanna d'Arco, Battaglio di Legnano, Luisa Miller*) and ballets within operas (*Il Trovatore, Macbeth, Ernani, Vespri Siciliani, Don Carlo*).⁹⁰

The musical pastiche is reminiscent of the Grand Radio Potpourri works which Burger created for the BBC. Reviews of *Vittorio* praise cast and company alike. Zachary Solov and Mia Slavenska (1916–2002) performed the lead roles with

---

85 "Burger and Hines, the fabulous comedy team of the Metropolitan Opera Company, for the second year in a row drew wild acclaim from a standing-room-only crowd in the Men's Quad dining room early Tuesday morning. They were the hit of the sixth annual After-Opera Antics, the Quad Hospitality Committee's informal reception for the 'Met' Company." Source: Nancy Harbin, Judy Miller, "Met Stars Thrill Audience in 'After-Opera Antics'," *The Indiana Daily Student*, 23 May 1956, Vol. LXXXV, No.151.

86 This version is part of the Jerome Hines Collection and resides in the Howard Gottlieb Archival Research Center at Boston University. Source: Julius Burger, *Legende (Christian Morgenstern)*, VI Musical Scores, Box 33, Folder 5, Number 67, Jerome Hines Collection -No.1263, Howard Gotlieb Archival Research Center, Boston University, 1998.

87 J.B., "Ingus Naruns heard in Recital on 'Cello," *The New York Times*, Vol. CII, No.34,586, 3 October, 1952, p.17. ;
    Arthur Berger, "Ingus Naruns: Latvian Cellist at Town Hall for a Return Recital," *New York Herald Tribune*, 3 October 1952.

88 Program for *Vittorio* at the Metropolitan Opera, New York, Playbill, 22 December 1954, p.10-11.

89 John Martin, "The Metropolitan Opera Presents a Ballet," *The New York Times*, 12 December 1954, Vol.CIV, No. 35,386, Section X, p.18.

90 Ibid, p.18.

Burger leads the orchestra in rehearsal at the Metropolitan Opera-NYC. Date Unknown. © A-Weaz

Burger in impromptu photo with friend – conductor Dimitri Mitropoulos – outside Metropolitan Opera, NYC. Late 1950s. © A-Weaz

Jean Lee Schoch as the gypsy fortune teller La Magilana, Judith Younger as Fiamma (the prince's fiancé) and Adriano Vitale, Edward Caton and Yurek Lazowski in character roles. One critic commented that *"[t]he orchestral arrangement was coordinated by Julius Burger, who performed a brilliant task in weaving the shreds of a patchwork into a beautiful mosaic of music. The score sounds as unified and fits the theme and mood of the story as if Verdi had composed it especially for last night's tour de force."*[91] The premiere also marked conductor Dimitri Mitropoulos's (1896–1960) debut with the Metropolitan Opera as well as his first engagement conducting a ballet. The collaboration led to a personal friendship between Mitropoulos and the Burgers, lasting until the conductor's death six years later.[92]

Two years later, in 1956, Burger was once again engaged outside his normal duties when he was approached to adapt and orchestrate the score for a new production of Jacques Offenbach's opera bouffe *La Périchole* (1868). The new English version was prepared by Jean Morel (1903–1975) and former Schreker student Ignace Strasfogel (1909–1994).[93] The production was directed by Cyril Ritchard (1898–1977) (who also performed the role of Don Andres), designed by Rolf Gérard (1909–2011) and choreographed by Zachary Solov. It starred coloratura soprano Patrice Munsel (1925–2016) in the title role.[94] In total, the production enjoyed fifty-three performances between 1956 and 1971. Its successful reception led to a commercial recording, released with RCA on their Victor Red Seal label,[95] a live telecast for NBC (26 January 1958)[96] and the score's publication with Boosey and Hawkes.[97]

While *La Périchole* marked a major success, Burger's final musical arrangement additions for the company's October

---

91 Thomas R. Dash, "'Vittorio' and 'Salome': Metropolitan Opera," *Women's Wear Daily*, 16 December 1954.

92 John Martin, "Solov's 'Vittorio' is danced at MET," *The New York Times*, 16 December 1954, Vol. CIV, No.35,390, p.49.

93 Both Morel and Strasfogel made their MET conducting debuts with this production- Morel with the work's premiere on 21 December 1956 and Strasfogel while the work was on tour on 6 May 1957 in Birmingham, Alabama. Sources: Jean Morel debut: "La Périchole," Performance 1, 21 December 1956, Metopera database, Metropolitan Opera Archives, CID: 173510, keyword search La Périchole, URL: http://archives.metoperafamily.org/archives/frame.htm, accessed 13 April 2021. ; Ignace Strasfogel debut: "La Périchole, Performance 16, 6 May 1957, Metopera database, Metropolitan Opera Archives, CID: 174990, keyword search La Périchole, URL: http://archives.metoperafamily.org/archives/frame.htm, accessed 13 April 2021.

94 This production was also Munsel's final engagement with the Metropolitan Opera. Her final performance was on 28 January 1958.

Source: "La Périchole," Performance 30, 28 January 1958, Metopera database, Metropolitan Opera Archives, CID: 176940, keyword search La Périchole, URL: http://archives.metoperafamily.org/archives/frame.htm, accessed 14 April 2021.

95 Jacques Offenbach, *La Périchole*, with the Metropolitan Opera Orchestra and Chorus, cond. by Jean Morel, RCA Victor Red Seal-LOC 1029, 1957, Vinyl LP.

96 The matinee telecast was broadcast from NBC Television studio in New York City as part of the Omnibus series. Source: "La Périchole," Performance 29, 26 January 1958, Metopera database, Metropolitan Opera Archives, CID: 176920, keyword search La Périchole, URL: http://archives.metoperafamily.org/archives/frame.htm, accessed 14 April 2021.

97 Jacques Offenbach "*La Périchole*," Metropolitan Opera version in English, Lyrics by Maurice Valency, vocal score revised/ adapted by Julius Burger, Boosey and Hawkes, Inc., New York, 1956.

Burger in playful discussion with friend – the American operatic Bass, Jerome Hines. 1950s. © A-Weaz

Burger with Hines performing a comedy skit at the AGMA Dinner. Biltmore Hotel-NYC. Summer 1952. © A-Weaz

1957 English language production of *Eugene Onegin* did not garner the same acclaim. The Peter Brook production was primed for success with set design by Rolf Gerard and choreography by Zachary Solov. The production also boasted a star studded cast including tenor Richard Tucker (1913–1975) as Lensky, Lucine Amara (b.1924) as Tatanya and baritone George London (1920–1985) in the title role.[98] The orchestra was presided over by Dimitri Mitropoulos who approached Burger to arrange four musical *entr'actes* for the production. The production ran for seventeen performances in its first season and while some critics positively acknowledged Burger's contributions, the overall production was slated as *"uninspired"*[99] and *"[l]ovely but dull"*.[100] Burger's *entr'actes* were later dropped from future revival productions.

Burger continued with the company for twenty years before retiring in 1969. Although a number of his compositions remain without dates of origin, an examination of his manuscript scores preserved in Exilarte shows a return to serious composition from 1967 onwards. There are several possible reasons for this sudden burst of creativity. It is likely he now had the financial means and time available to rekindle his former career, freed from juggling multiple jobs at once as he had done for the previous thirty years. This period shows a new concerted effort at composition with a particular focus on lieder, instrumental chamber works and numerous examples of instrumental and vocal arrangements. Equally, there is evidence Burger continued to revise earlier compositions during this late period.

The process of dating is made difficult as many late works possess little or no indications of chronology. Manuscripts which have been dated reveal Burger composed at least two string quartets (No. 2 and No. 3, both 1968), several orchestrated lieder, multiple arrangements of existing works for voice, solo piano, and instrumental chamber ensembles. The period (from 1967 to 1988) includes at least eighteen dated lieder for voice and piano (including two sets of four lieder each, *Lieder des Alters* (1970) and *Vier Heitere Lieder* (1979)). Interestingly, all of his lieder with the exception of two – *Nobody* (1988) and *The Long Furrow* (Undated) – are settings of German text. This could be interpreted as an indicator of his strong identification with Austro-Germanic culture of earlier life despite decades of exile.

Aside from composing in his retirement, Burger also continued to regularly coach prominent singers from his Queens apartment and made annual holiday trips to Europe, particularly Austria. It is clear from his correspondence in the 1970s and 1980s, now preserved in Exilarte, Burger was driven to rekindle his career as a composer. One clear example of this is a response from the office of pre-eminent lied interpreter and baritone Dietrich Fischer-Dieskau regarding Burger's *Vier Heitere Lieder*. After reviewing the work, a recommendation of the collection from the famed singer was then forwarded with a copy of the work to a contact at Burger's former publisher, Musikverlag Cranz, for consideration. However, there is no indication this was successful.

98 "Eugene Onegin," 28 October 1957, Metropera database, Metropolitan Opera Archives, CID: 176000, keyword search Eugene Onegin, URL: http://archives.metoperafamily.org/archives/frame.htm, accessed 14 April 2021.

99 John Chapman, "Metropolitan Opera bows with an uninspired 'Eugene Onegin'", *New York Daily News*, 29 October 1957, p.50.

100 Miles Kastendieck, "'Eugene Onegin' Lovely but Dull," *New York Journal-American*, 29 October 1957, in the Burger Collection, Exilarte Zentrum Archiv der mdw, Vienna, Austria.

Julius and Rose in the park. Circa 1980s. © A-Weaz

A later attempt at garnering a performance of a different work proved to be more successful. In 1984, aged 87, Burger's orchestral work *Variations on a Theme by Carl Phillipp Emanuel Bach* (1945) gained first prize at Indiana State University's Contemporary Music Festival Competition. The work was premiered by the Indianapolis Symphony Orchestra on 27 September 1984 in Tilson Music Hall on the university's campus. This marked the first public performance of any of Burger's non-commissioned works in thirty-two years.[101]

Five years later, Burger's personal life suffered a major blow when on 25 April 1989, Rose Burger died. The couple were married for nearly 56 years. A little over a year later, in June 1990, Burger made contact with New York probate attorney Ronald S. Pohl, Esq. to settle his and his wife's estates. Through initial conversations, Pohl was regaled with stories of Burger's life and impressive career and equally, the composer's desire to hear selections from his own large œuvre before he died. The stacks of manuscript scores had now been sitting relatively untouched in the composer's Queens apartment for years. After making contact with professional musicians in New York on Burger's behalf, Pohl initiated the revival of the composer's music with a concert on 3 June 1991 in Alice Tully Hall in the Lincoln Centre, New York.[102] Other orchestral concerts followed, including performances of orchestral selections with the New Orchestra of Westchester in Purchase, New York,[103] the University of Negev in Beersheba, Israel and the Austin Symphony in Texas.[104]

Despite ailing health, Burger flew to Berlin in September 1994 to attend recording sessions and a concert performance of his works in Berlin's Jesus Christus Kirche. This was his first visit to the city since leaving in 1933. The repertoire comprised selections of his orchestral works, performed by Rundfunk Sinfonieorchester Berlin and conducted by Simone Young.[105] The recordings were later released commercially

---

101 Julius Burger, "Variations on a Theme by C.P.E. Bach," Playbill for Contemporary Music Festival - Indiana State University (1984), Indianapolis Symphony Orchestra, Dir. by John Nelson, William Henry Curry, Tilson Music Hall, Indiana State University, 27 September 1984.
   A copy of the original programme is included in the Julius Burger Collection, Exilarte Zentrum Archiv der mdw, Vienna, Austria.

102 The concert included the New York premiere of his *Variations on a Theme by Carl Phillipp Emanuel Bach* (1945), *Concerto for Cello and Orchestra* (1932) and the world premieres of his *Symphonic Scherzo for String Orchestra* (1937), *Zigeunerlied for Violin and Piano* (Undated) and the *Eastern Symphony* (1931, Berlin). Source: "The Orchestra of St. Luke's perform the works of Julius Burger," Lincoln Center Stage bill, June 1991, p.13-16B, 33.

103 This concert featured a performance of Burger's *Eastern Symphony* conducted by Paul Lustig Dunkel in SUNY / Purchase College's Performing Arts Center on 23 and 24 October 1993. Source: "New Orchestra of Westchester's Eleventh Concert Season 1993-94", Stage bill for The Eleventh Season 1993–1994, Performing Arts Center SUNY/Purchase, Purchase, New York, p.O-3 - O-5

104 The concert featured works by Burger on the 2nd and 3rd of December 1994 in Austin, Texas.
   Source: Jerry Young, "Burger finally hears his music with Austin Symphony," *Austin American-Statesman*, Entertainment section, 28 November 1994, p.B8.

105 The concert was held at the Jesus-Christus-Kirche in Berlin on 29 September 1994 and included performances of the *Scherzo for String Orchestra* (1937), the orchestral lieder *Legende* (1919) & *Stille der Nacht* (1923) which are known as *Two Songs for Baritone and Orchestra* with vocalist Michael Kraus, *Concerto for Cello and Orchestra* (1932) with soloist Maya Beiser and *Variations on a Theme by Carl Phillipp Emanuel Bach* (1945). Source: Julius Burger, "Konzert mit Werken von Julius Bürger," Stagebill, Rundfunk-Sinfonieorchester Berlin, Maya Beiser, cello, Michael Kraus, baritone, cond. Simone Young, Jesus Christus Kirche, Berlin, 29 September 1994.

Julius Burger and Ronald S. Pohl, Esq. © Brian Coats, All Rights Reserved.

on the Toccata Classics label in 2007. More recently, a large portion of his lieder for voice and piano were recorded by Dutch-American baritone Ryan Hugh Ross for commercial release on the Spätlese Musik label. The album was released in November 2019.

Julius Burger died in New York City on 12 June 1995, roughly nine months following the Berlin sessions. He was 98.[106]

His estate, including his personal papers and manuscripts, was maintained by his friend and attorney, Ronald S. Pohl, Esq. until 2016 when they were given on permanent loan to the Exilarte Zentrum Archiv in Vienna for preservation and research purposes.

---

[106] "Julius Burger, A Conductor, Dies," *New York Times*, 15 June 1995, URL: https://nyti.ms/3fXIHgC, Accessed 02 January 2022.

Julius Burger awaiting the Lincoln Centre World Premiere concert comprising of selections from his orchestral œuvre. Alice Tully Hall, Lincoln Centre. New York NY. 3 June 1991. © A-Weaz

Burger points to a poster advertising his grand revival concert at Alice Tully Hall, Lincoln Centre, performed by The Orchestra of St. Lukes. June 1991. © A-Weaz

3. JULIUS BURGER'S OPUS

3.1 Instrumental Music (Catalogue 1.1.)

3.1.1 Chamber music (Catalogue 1.1.2.)

Burger's compositional œuvre includes an array of chamber works for a variety of instrumentation. While not all works are dated, many originate from the 1930s onward and show a trajectory moving away from larger orchestral forms toward compositions for small ensembles and voice. This is particularly true of his late composition period (1967–1988) which, aside from small reworking, is void of the larger orchestral forms of the early period. Several significant examples of Burger's mastery of the art of arranging include his work for piano titled *Paganini* (Box 1, No. 1.1.1.1) and for small string ensemble (*Three Studies for Pianoforte by Chopin*). The work, arranged for violin I and II, cello, and bass, incorporates Chopin's works for solo keyboard including his op. 10, no. 6; op. 10, no. 7; and op. 25, no. 9. Burger's version stems from the early 1940s when he was employed an arranger with CBS in New York City.[107]

Several arrangements for violin and piano are also preserved from the estate including his sumptuous treatment of Antonín Dvořák's *Serenade* from his *Poetické nálady* for piano, Op. 85, No. 9 (Box 1, No. 1.1.2.2.1.)[108] as well as a setting of the 1930 work *Zigeunerlied*, also for violin and piano (Box 6, No. 1.1.3.1.2.4. – 12.).[109] These works show an affinity for the composers and musical traditions of Eastern Europe, a theme which occurs frequently in his orchestral and chamber works. Other noteworthy works in this category include the *Family Serenade* which, according to the inscription, was composed for the Klein Brothers. It is scored for flute/piccolo and two French horns (Box 1, No. 1.1.2.3.1.).

Of his chamber works, several stand out from the rest for their originality as well as their jarring compositional style. These are his three string quartets. While the first is not dated and only remains in a manuscript part for cello (*String Quartet No. 1*; Box 1, No. 1.1.2.4.1.), his second and third string quartets are an example of Burger's versatility, ability and willingness to experiment with traditional harmonic tonalities. *String Quartet, No.2* (1968) (Box 1, No. 1.1.2.4.2.) holds

---

107 Julius Burger, Letter to Stanford Robinson, 17 May 1943, from Burger, Julius, '42-'51. R27/40/2. Music-General. File Folder II of II. BBC Written Archives Centre, Caversham – England.

108 This setting of *Serenade* has also been arranged for a small ensemble; Flute, Horns (2 part), Oboe, Clarinet (2 part), and Bassoon (2 part). Source: Julius Burger, *Serenade*, arrangement of Antonin Dvořák's op.85, no.9 for Flute, Oboe, 2 Clarinets, 2 Bassoons and 2 Horns, Eaz-001-03-00022 – 00026, Box 1, No. 1.1.2.2.1., Julius Burger (Bürger) Collection, Exilarte Zentrum Archiv der mdw, Vienna, Austria.

109 *Zigeunerlied* also exists as an arrangement for Violin and Orchestra. Source: Julius Burger, *Zigeunerlied* for Violin and Orchestra, Eaz-001-03-00064 – 00120, Box 6 – 7, No. 1.1.3.1.2. – 15., Julius Burger (Bürger) Collection, Exilarte Zentrum Archiv der mdw, Vienna, Austria.

Burger's 2nd *String Quartet* (1968)
© A-Weaz

to the standard, four movement quartet structure (I. Allegro, II. Larghetto, III. Allegro moderato – presto, IV. Andante) but displays an impressively unique style and language that differs from his previous examples of this œuvre which are generally grounded in Fin de siècle Romanticism.

Burger's *String Quartet No. 3* (1968) (Box 2, No. 1.1.2.4.3.) also exhibits a desire to experiment with less traditional styles. The work also does away with traditional quartet practices of sonata form by only incorporating three movements (I. Allegro moderato, II. Adagio, III. Vivace scherzoso). Both works lean toward stylistic tendencies reminiscent of string quartets by Second Viennese School composer Alban Berg (such as his Streichquartett, Op. 3, 1925–6), Alexander Zemlinsky (Streichquartett No. 4, 1936) whose later works incorporated elements of neoclassicism, Jazz and *Neue Sachlichkeit*, or the string quartets of Erwin Schulhoff (String Quartet, No. 1 (1924) and String Quartet, No. 2 (1925)).

As is the case with the rest of the Burger catalogue, these works remain in manuscript form and unpublished. They were first performed on 1 May 1991 in a chamber concert sponsored by the America-Israel Cultural Foundation as part of the first revival concerts of the composer's music.[110] In recent years there has been a renewed interest in the string quartets with musical ensembles such as the Vienna-based Adamas Quartett, who performed the work in 2017.[111]

3.1.2 Orchestral works (Catalogue 1.1.3.)

Burger's orchestral works and arrangements hold particular importance in his œuvre, acting as a showcase for the quality of his craftsmanship and abilities in composing for larger forces. Equally, they showcase an individualised compositional voice influenced by early-twentieth century Austro-German composers such as Alexander Zemlinsky and Joseph Marx while drawing on the diatonic lyricism of Erich Korngold, Richard Strauss as well as stylistic elements from his former teacher Franz Schreker.[112]

Nearly all Burger's orchestral compositions can be attributed to his early creative period between 1915 and 1939. The vast majority were conceived and written primarily whilst he was based in Berlin and his early years of exile (the London period of 1933 to 1939). Several pieces extend into his first years

---

110 The concert included premiere performances of the String Quartets No.2 & No.3 (1968), and the arrangements of *Serenade for Violin and Piano* (Dvořák op.85, No.9) as well as *Zigeunerlied for Violin and Piano*. Source: Chamber Concert with music by Julius Burger, feat. Mannes College Quartet, Catherine French, violin, Indira Koch, violin, Matthew Rombaum, viola, Kathleen Melucci, cello, America-Israeli Cultural Foundation, New York City, NY, 1 May 1991.

111 *Streichquartett, No.2* (1968) by Julius Burger, performed by the Adamas String Quartett,, Gesprächskonzert- Exilarte Zentrum der mdw, Clara Schumann-Saal, Universität für Musik und darstellende Kunst Wien, 18 May 2017.

112 Malcolm MacDonald, "Julius Burger (1897–1995): Orchestral Music," Liner Notes, Radio Symphonie Orchester, Berlin, cond. Simone Young, recorded 26-28,30 September 1994, Toccata Classics, TOCC 0001, 2007, CD, p.5.

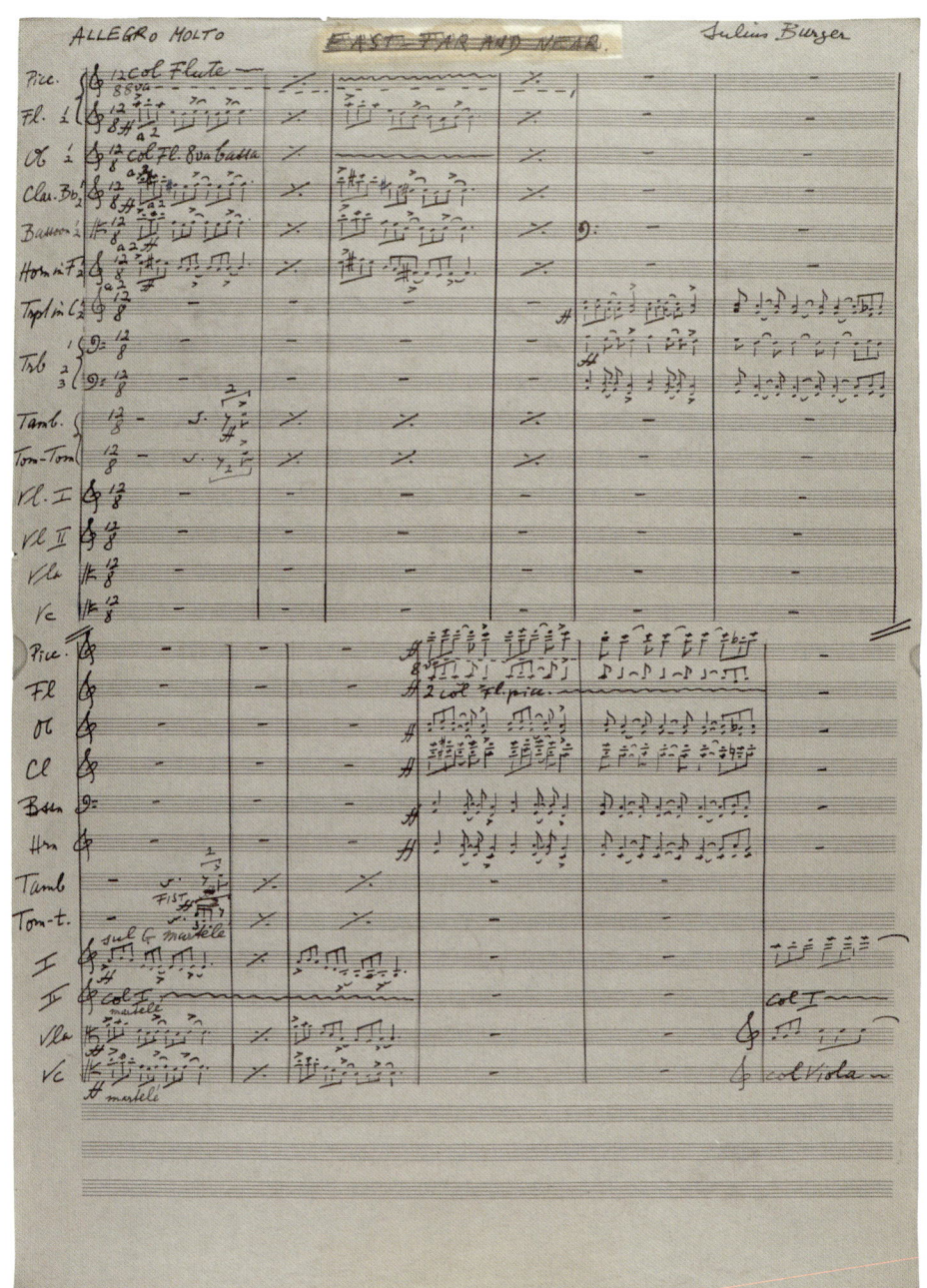

The opening measures to Burger's electric *Eastern Symphony* (titled *East – Far and Near*). © A-Weaz

of exile in New York, including the completion of his *Variations on a Theme by Carl Philipp Emanuel Bach* in 1945.[113] Current research concludes Burger did not compose any exclusively large-scale orchestral works after this date.

Burger's orchestral works are not concentrated in any one form but instead draw on multiple genres which show his compositional prowess. Prominent examples include a symphony in three movements *Eastern Symphony* (Box 11-13, No. 1.1.3.4.3.), the *Concerto for Cello and Orchestra* (Box 3-5, No. 1.1.3.1.1.), at least two works for string ensemble including *Symphonic Scherzo for Strings* (Box 8-9, No. 1.1.3.2.1.) and *Adagio for Strings "The Last Goodbye"* (Box 10, No. 1.1.3.2.3.) as well as the *Variations on a Theme by Carl Phillipp Emanuel Bach* (Box 14-16, No. 1.1.3.5.3.).

Other works include an arrangement of the *Zigeunerlied* for violin and orchestra (Box 6-7, No. 1.1.3.1.2.) and at least three orchestral suites. These two arranged works for strings – *First Suite of Four Classic Songs* (Box 10, No. 1.1.3.3.2.) and *Second Suite of Classic Songs* (Box 10, No. 1.1.3.3.3.) – are comprised of orchestrated songs by Hugo Wolf, Franz Schubert, Robert Schumann, Johannes Brahms, and Richard Strauss.[114] A further suite, titled *Suite of Five Little Pieces from Vienna* (Box 11, No. 1.1.3.4.1.), creates a musical portrait of Vienna in five vignettes titled 'Schubert's Geburtshaus' (I), 'Ballet am Opernring' (II), 'Changing of the Guard at the Burg-Ring' (III), 'In Grinzing' (IV) and 'Karusell im Prater' (V).[115]

Burger's earliest known orchestral work *Ozeanfahrt, 1925* (für Großes Orchester) was a symphonic overture described by Burger as "modern but full of melody and describes the impressions of a modern ocean trip."[116] The date in the title indicates he may have been inspired to compose the work when travelling between his apprenticeship at the Metropolitan Opera and Europe. It was performed by the Berlin Funk-Orchester and broadcast at 9.15PM on 22 April 1931 as part of an orchestral concert conducted by Bruno Seidler-Winkler.[117] Unfortunately, the location of this manuscript is not known.

---

113 Lynne S. Mazza, "The Orchestra of St. Luke's perform the music of Julius Burger," Program notes for Eastern Symphony, The Orchestra of St. Luke's, cond. Paul Lustig Dunkel, New York: Alice Tully Hall, 3 June 1991, p.14.

114 *First Suite of Four Classic Songs* includes orchestrated settings of Hugo Wolf (*Auch kleine Dinge - Italienisches Liederbuch (1892)*), Franz Schubert (*Auf dem Wasser zu Singen* Op.72, D.774 (1823)), Robert Schumann (*Mondnacht – Liederkreis* Op.39, No.5, (1840)) and Johannes Brahms (*Ständchen* Op.106, No.1 (1885)). The Second Suite of Four Classic Songs, also orchestrated for strings, includes settings of works by Franz Schubert (*Der Jungling an der Quelle*, D.300 (1817), Hugo Wolf (*Der Gärtner*, No.17 from *Mörike Lieder* (1888), Richard Strauss (*Freundliche Vision*, Op.48, No.1 (1900) and Johannes Brahms (*Vergebliches Ständchen*, Op.84, No.4 (1881)).

Source: Julius Burger, "Composition list," from personal papers held in the private collection of Dr. Trude Zörer, Vienna, Austria, p.75.

115 This suite was premiered on the BBC National Service by the BBC Theatre Orchestra, conducted by Stanford Robinson, on 14 December 1937 at 10:20PM. Sources: Contributor, " Suite of Five Little Pieces of Vienna," *Radio Times*, Vol.57, Issue 741, p.44. ; Julius Burger, "Composition list", from personal papers held in the private collection of Dr. Trude Zörer, Vienna, Austria, p.74.

116 Julius Burger, "Letter to the BBC-London," 27 April 1931, From Burger, Julius. 31-42. R27/40/2. BBC Music-General: Burger, Julius. BBC Written Archives Centre, Reading, England.

117 Berlin Funk-Stunde programme list for Wednesday 22 April 1931, From Burger, Julius. 31-42. R27/40/2. BBC Music-General: Burger, Julius. BBC Written Archives Centre, Reading, England.

Burger progressed from his symphonic overture onto progressively larger works including the *Eastern Symphony* (previously titled "Near and Far"). The work is more reminiscent of a tone poem in three movements rather than a setting in the traditional symphonic structure, which utilises four movements. The work's characteristic use of modalities provides a soundscape which is decidedly non-Western and hints at Burger's connection with Eastern European traditions as a possible inspiration. This is then coupled with other thematic material seemingly from outside of Western classical traditions.[118] Each of the three movements offers a distinctive vignette in which Burger utilises particular instrumentation to great effect. Burger began the work in 1931 and it was later completed in 1935 while he was actively involved as a composer and arranger for the BBC's Variety Department.[119]

The *Concerto for Cello and Orchestra* (1932) also originates in the early compositional period and was later revised over the following decades.[120] The piece shows Burger's affinity for the cello's uniquely expressive capabilities and warm, voice-like tonal colours. It is possible this interest in the cello stems from his lessons on the instrument while enrolled at the Academy in Vienna between in the latter half of the 1910s.[121] The concerto was first premiered in a reduced arrangement for cello (performed by Latvian-born Ingus Naruns) and two pianos (performed by Anatolijis Berzkahlns and Burger) at the Town Hall in New York City on 2 October 1952.[122] Notably, it was Ingus Naruns who added the unaccompanied cadenza later incorporated into the third movement.[123] The performance was reviewed by several prominent newspapers of the period including the *New York Times*, the *New York Herald Tribune* as well as the German language publication the *New Yorker Staats-Zeitung*.[124] The original, fully orchestrat-

---

118 Lynne S. Mazza, "The Orchestra of St. Luke's perform the music of Julius Burger," Program notes for *Eastern Symphony*, The Orchestra of St. Luke's, cond. Paul Lustig Dunkel, New York: Alice Tully Hall, 3 June 1991, p.16-16A.

119 The *Eastern Symphony* was premiered on 3 June 1991 at 8PM at Alice Tully Hall in Lincoln Center in New York City by Paul Lustig Dunkel conducting the Orchestra of St. Luke's in a programme comprised entirely of works by Julius Burger. Other compositions receiving their premieres include the Variations on a Theme by Carl Phillipp Emanuel Bach (New York Premiere), *Concerto for Cello and Orchestra*, *Symphonic Scherzo for String Orchestra* (World Premiere) and *Zigeunerlied for Violin and Orchestra* (World Premiere). Source: "The Orchestra of St. Luke's perform the music of Julius Burger," Program notes for Eastern Symphony, The Orchestra of St. Luke's, cond. Paul Lustig Dunkel, New York: Alice Tully Hall, 3 June 1991.

120 "The Orchestra of St. Luke's perform the music of Julius Burger," Program notes for Eastern Symphony, The Orchestra of St. Luke's, cond. Paul Lustig Dunkel, New York: Alice Tully Hall, 3 June 1991; Julius Burger, "Composition list," from personal papers held in the private collection of Dr. Trude Zörer, Vienna, Austria, p.75.

121 Julius Bürger Enrollment document from Akademie für Musik und darstellende Kunst Wien, Matrikel Nr.(285), 1917/18; 1918/19.

122 Arthur Berger, "Ingus Naruns: Latvian Cellist at Town Hall for a Return Recital," *New York Times*, 3 October 1952, Vol. CII.., No. 34,586, p.17.

123 Julius Burger, "Composition list," from personal papers held in the private collection of Dr. Trude Zörer, Vienna, Austria, p.44.

124 *Staats-Zeitung* Critic Fred Low lauded the three movement as "…die drei Sätze sind in Erfindung und Durchführung bemerkenswert und sowohl die lyrischen Passagen des Adagio wie die technisch schwierig zu spielenden Stellen des Finale zeigen den erfahrenen Komponisten." (remarkable in invention and development and both the lyrical passages of the adagio and the technically difficult passages of the finale show an experienced composer.) Source: Fred Low, "Aus der Musikwelt," *New Yorker Staats-Zeitung*, October 1952. From Julius Burger Collection, Exilarte Zentrum der mdw, Vienna, Austria.

ed version did not receive its premiere for another 39 years when it was performed at the June 1991 Alice Tully Hall Concert in New York.[125]

The concerto follows the traditional, three movement form full of vocal lyricism and holds an expressive warmth throughout. It is orchestrated for cello soloist, woodwind, brass, and strings with the addition of harp, timpani, and xylophone. The Allegro movement is episodic. It opens with a brief Adagio introduction which utilises the breadth of the cello's range before developing into a theme defined by chains of rising and descending fourths.[126] This theme is central to the work and returns in the coda of the first movement as well as in the final Allegro vivace movement.

The second movement, Adagio in B-flat minor, is soulful, solemn, and expressive with what could be interpreted as Hebraic musical influences throughout.[127] Burger reintroduces the chains of descending fourths in the timpani against undulating strings, giving the movement a solemn atmosphere. The movement develops these elements with a continued reiteration of the melody of increasing intensity before giving way to a final reprise of opening theme in the cello, as the undulating strings, timpani and harp drift the movement into silence. It is evident this movement held particular significance to Burger as he dedicated it "to the memory of my mother who at the age of 78 years was murdered on September 28, 1942, in Auschwitz."[128] The immensely emotive movement is poignant tribute to her memory.

The final movement, Allegro vivace in F major, is in an ABAB form with the A form 'vivace' music returning to the first movement's original subject. The B form develops a new tune for cello and strings, eventually leading in its second appearance to the unaccompanied cadenza before a short display by the orchestra to conclude the piece.

Other works focus more exclusively on the capabilities of the string section. Two examples include the aforementioned works *Symphonic Scherzo for Strings* (1939) and the *Adagio for Strings*, also known as "The Last Goodbye". The *Symphonic Scherzo for Strings* was not completed until the late 1930s and was first developed as a string quartet.[129] An early sketch of the melody in triple meter was apparently shared

---

125 "The Orchestra of St. Luke's perform the works of Julius Burger," Lincoln Center Stagebill, June 1991, p.13-16B, 33.

126 Malcolm MacDonald, "Julius Burger (1897–1995): Orchestral Music," Liner Notes, Radio Symphonie Orchester, Berlin, cond. Simone Young, recorded 26-28,30 September 1994, Toccata Classics, TOCC 0001, 2007, CD, p.7.

127 Ibid., p.7.

128 Julius Burger, *Konzert für Violoncello und Orchester* (1932), [EaZ-001-03-00108], Box 6, No.1.1.3.2.2., Julius Burger (Bürger) Collection, Exilarte Zentrum Archiv der mdw, Vienna, Austria.

129 There are conflicting composition dates for this work with scarcity of primary source material for confirmation. The Toccata Classics release of Burger's orchestral works lists 1939 while the programme notes for the June 1991 Alice Tully Hall lists the work as completed in 1937. More research is necessary to confirm its origins. Sources: Malcolm MacDonald, "Julius Burger (1897–1995): Orchestral Music," Liner Notes, Radio Symphonie Orchester, Berlin, cond. Simone Young, recorded 26-28,30 September 1994, Toccata Classics, TOCC 0001, 2007, CD, p.7.;

Lynne S. Mazza, "The Orchestra of St. Luke's perform the music of Julius Burger," Program notes for Eastern Symphony, The Orchestra of St. Luke's, cond. Paul Lustig Dunkel, New York: Alice Tully Hall, 3 June 1991, p.15.

Promotional photo for the 3 October 1952 New York Town Hall recital which featured a reduced arrangement of Burger's *Concerto for Cello and Orchestra*. Burger pictured with Latvian cellist Ingus Naruns. © A-Weaz

with Franz Schreker who commented it was evocative of "music with fire."[130] The work is forceful and invigorating, opening with a three-note motif in F minor. This is continually reasserted and developed throughout the piece. The D minor development section reveals a second subject before passing onto an E minor fugato. The concluding section then combines the two themes into a frenzied climax before ending the piece utilising an unrelenting reintroduction of the three-note motif. The work displays Burger's sophisticated knowledge of string instrumentation, use harmonic structures and rhythmic devices for an impressive display.

Perhaps the work which displays the composer's mastery of form more than any other is his *Variations on a Theme by Carl Philipp Emanuel Bach* (1945). Burger commenced on the work in 1933 in Berlin but did not complete it until after he was living in New York City in 1945.[131] This work reveals Burger's wide-ranging knowledge of musical styles and traditions. Equally, it is characterful, displaying an immense palette of orchestral colours which have been imaginatively crafted into a single comprehensive piece. It should also be noted that this piece won first prize at Indiana State University's Contemporary Music Festival Competition in 1984.[132] Its premiere by the Indianapolis Symphony Orchestra on 27 September of that year marks one of the few public performances of any of his œuvre before his revival in the early 1990s.

The work opens with a respectful treatment of C. P. E. Bach's main theme, marked Andante grazioso, before progressing through eleven variations. The first variation, *Energico*, eludes to a modern twentieth century soundscape with violin solo. This then progresses to the boisterous *Allegro moderato* (v. II) to the solemn *Lento* (v.III). A mercurial *Presto alla breve* (v.IV) leads to a stylistically Romantic *Giusto tempo* in A flat (v. V) before a trumpet and piano open the *Vivace* variation (v. VI) with a playful presentation reminiscent of vaudeville music or the folk tune quotations in Aaron Copland's *Hoedown* (v. IV) from his 1942 symphonic suite *Rodeo*. The *Andante sostenuto* in E flat (v. VII) enters a full cinematic display of lush music reminiscent of Burger's Viennese contemporary, Erich Korngold[133] before moving onto the thematically light march in C *Allegretto, grazioso* (v. VIII) led by woodwinds and triangle with brass interjections.

An aggressive *Allegro* in E minor (v. IX) enters before concluding with a piano solo reminiscent of Burger's original treatment of the main theme. A nocturne *Adagio* (v. X) in

---

130 Lynne S. Mazza, "The Orchestra of St. Luke's perform the music of Julius Burger," Program notes for Eastern Symphony, The Orchestra of St. Luke's, cond. Paul Lustig Dunkel, New York: Alice Tully Hall, 3 June 1991, p.16.

131 Sources: Julius Burger, "Composition list", from personal papers held in the private collection of Dr. Trude Zörer, Vienna, Austria, p42. ;

Lynne S. Mazza, "The Orchestra of St. Luke's perform the music of Julius Burger," Program notes for *Variations on a Theme by Carl Philipp Emanuel Bach*, The Orchestra of St. Luke's, cond. Paul Lustig Dunkel, New York: Alice Tully Hall, 3 June 1991, p.14.

132 Julius Burger, "Variations on a Theme by C.P.E. Bach," Playbill for Contemporary Music Festival – Indiana State University (1984), Indianapolis Symphony Orchestra, Dir. by John Nelson, William Henry Curry, Tilson Music Hall, Indiana State University, 27 September 1984.

A copy of the original programme is included in the Julius Burger Collection, Exilarte Zentrum Archiv der mdw, Vienna, Austria.

133 Malcolm MacDonald, "Julius Burger (1897–1995): Orchestral Music," Liner Notes, Radio Symphonie Orchester, Berlin, cond. Simone Young, recorded 26-28, 30 September 1994, Toccata Classics, TOCC 0001, 2007, CD, p.10.

E major opens with a string quartet, arpeggiated harp and woodwinds before peaking with full orchestra. It concludes with a coda in elegant fashion reminiscent of Burger's treatment of the main theme.[134] Burger then draws on the expanse of the orchestra to show his technical skill in an impressive display for the eleventh *Presto* variation titled 'Scherzo'. The piece then ends with full orchestra in regal fashion in the Coda (*Solenne*).

Additionally, other notable compositions in this category include *A Musical Jest with Johann Strauss*[135] (Box 14, No. 1.1.3.4.4.) written for orchestra, celeste and harp as well as the 1942 work *Roumanian Fantasy* (Box 14, No. 1.1.3.5.2.). The latter was recorded by Andre Kostelanetz in 1944 on the Columbia Masterworks label.[136] Several letters preserved in the BBC Written Archives trace the origins of this work and Burger's frustration with Kostelanetz for not receiving credit as composer and arranger on the commercial recording.[137] This is an exciting piece which utilises thematic material from Romanian folk tunes arranged for orchestra and shares similarities with George Enescu's Rhapsodies composed in 1901 (*Romanian Rhapsody No. 1* in A major, op. 11 and *Romanian Rhapsody No. 2* in D major, op. 11). Fortunately, this work is preserved in manuscript as part of the Exilarte's Julius Burger (Bürger) collection.

---

134 Ibid., p.10.

135 This work was most likely completed in Burger's first years in New York City post 1939. Letters between Burger and former BBC colleague Stanford Robinson preserved at the BBC Written Archives, Caversham, England show Burger had sent the work for performance consideration on the BBC but these were eventually returned and were not broadcast. Source: Julius Burger, "Letter to Stanford Robinson," 17 May 1943, From Burger, Julius. '42-'51. R27/40/2. BBC Music-General: Burger, Julius. BBC Written Archives Centre, Reading, England.

136 The recording of this work is listed as: "November 26, 1944 - XCO-33901/02. TRADITIONAL: *Roumanian Fantasy* (Gypsy Songs) (5:34) 78s: Columbia 7427-M. 45s: 4-7427-M. LPs: AAL-4 (also labelled AL-4). Source: James H. North, *Andre Kostelanetz on Records and on the Air: A Discography and Radio Log*, (Lanham: Scarecrow Press, 2010). p.10.

137 Additionally, one letter from February 1945 notes *Roumanian Fantasy* was reportedly admired by conductor Arturo Toscanini who inquired about a possible performance. However, after Burger was left off as the arranger, he took it upon himself to write Toscanini of the situation. The result was Toscanini performed Enescu's *Romanian Rhapsody* No.1 shortly thereafter.

Source: Julius Burger, "Letter to Stanford Robinson," 22 February 1945, From Burger, Julius. '42-'51. R27/40/2. BBC Music-General: Burger, Julius. BBC Written Archives Centre, Reading, England.

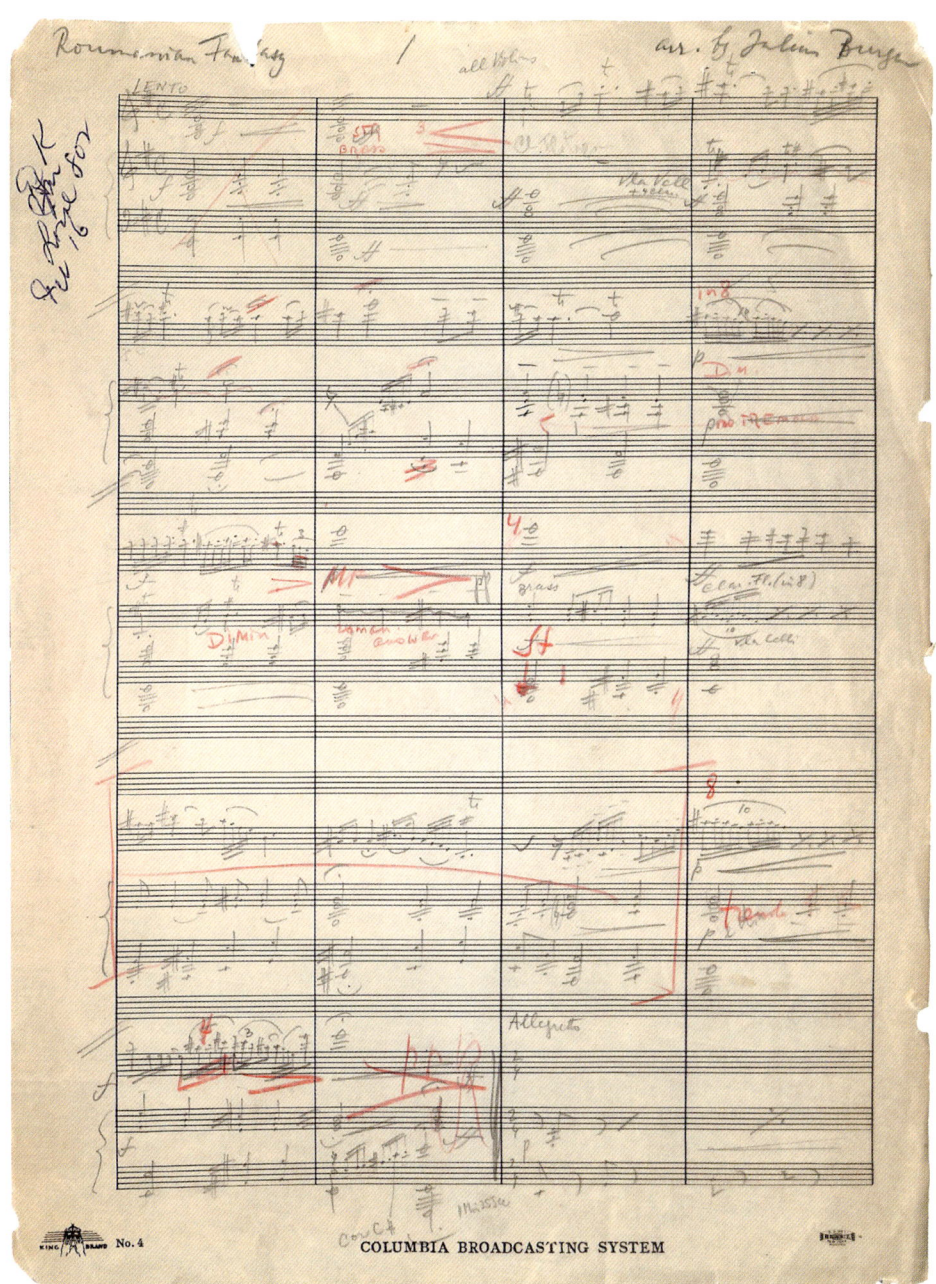

Manuscript for Julius Burger's *Roumanian Fantasy* (1942). The work was composed for and recorded by conductor Andre Kostelanetz on the Columbia Masterworks label.
© A-Weaz

3.2 Vocal Music (Catalogue 1.2.)

3.2.1 Voice and Piano (Catalogue 1.2.1.: Box 17, No. 1.2.1.1. – 1.2.1.23.)

In an interview titled "Burger finally hears his music with Austin Symphony" for the *Austin American-Statesman* newspaper, reporter Jerry Young asked Julius Burger if there were many regrets about giving up orchestral composing during the past fifty years. Burger replied *"Now, yes – definitely. But I never stopped composing Lieder."*[138]

This statement highlights the importance of Burger's compositions in the genre which span 73 years from his earliest known lied in 1915 (*Dämmernd liegt der Sommerabend*; text by H. Heine) to his final two lieder composed in 1988 (*Nobody* and *Goodbye, Vienna*; text by J. Burger). While Burger's orchestral compositions and arrangements show his mastery over the larger forms, his vocal compositions, with selections for orchestral as well as piano accompaniment, are equally worthy contributions. Selections of these have been scored for the core vocal fachs and frequently rely on the expanse of the vocal range. Most of these works are written for voice and piano with an additional nine lieder scored for orchestral accompaniment.

Four lieder were originally composed for orchestral accompaniment including *Legende* (c. 1919, text by C. Morgenstern),[139] *Stille der Nacht* (c. 1923, text by G. Keller),[140] *Zigeunerlied* (c. 1930, text by R. Kessler) and *Launisches Glück* (c.1932, text by L. Hainisch).[141] Three others with orchestral accompaniment, including *Schlummerlied* (undated, text by A. Mombert)[142], *So Tanze meine Seele* (1968, text by A. Von Halzfeld)[143] and *Venedig* (1970, text by F. Nietzsche)[144] were rescored from their vocal and piano formats in 1985. Two other works, *Verbogenheit* (arr. after 1940, from *Mörike Lieder*, No. 12, 1888)[145] and *In dem Schatten meiner Locken*

---

138 Jerry Young, "Burger finally hears his music with Austin Symphony," *Austin American-Statesman*, November 1994, Entertainment section B8, p.28.

139 Julius Burger, *Legende* (1919), for baritone and orchestra with text by Christian Morgenstern, EaZ-001-03-00223 – 00230, Box 18, No. 1.2.3.2., Julius Burger (Bürger) Collection, Exilarte Zentrum Archiv der mdw, Vienna, Austria.

140 Julius Burger, *Stille der Nacht* (1923), for baritone and orchestra with text by Gottfried Keller, EaZ-001-03-00289 – 00350, Box 19, No. 1.2.3.3., Julius Burger (Bürger) Collection, Exilarte Zentrum Archiv der mdw, Vienna, Austria.

141 Locations Unknown

142 Julius Burger, *Schlummerlied* for voice and orchestra with text by Alfred Mombert, EaZ-001-03-00527 – 00529, Box 20, No. 1.2.3.4., Julius Burger (Bürger) Collection, Exilarte Zentrum Archiv der mdw, Vienna, Austria.

143 Julius Burger, *So Tanze meine Seele* (1985) for voice and orchestra with text by Adolf von Hatzfeld, EaZ-001-03-005530 – 00531, Box 18, No. 1.2.3.1., Julius Burger (Bürger) Collection, Exilarte Zentrum Archiv der mdw, Vienna, Austria.

144 Julius Burger, *Venedig* (1985) for voice and orchestra with text by Friedrich Nietzsche, EaZ-001-03-00512 – 00513, Box 20, No. 1.2.3.5., Julius Burger (Bürger) Collection, Exilarte Zentrum Archiv der mdw, Vienna, Austria.

145 Julius Burger, *Verborgenheit* – a setting of the Hugo Wolf piece for voice and orchestra with text by Eduard Mörike, EaZ-001-03-00532, Box 22, No. 1.2.4.1., Julius Burger (Bürger) Collection, Exilarte Zentrum Archiv der mdw, Vienna, Austria.

(arr. after 1940, from *Spanisches Liederbuch: Weltliche Lieder*, No. 12, 1890)[146] are arrangements of lieder by Hugo Wolf. A further defining feature of the lieder works stems from Burger's text choices. He almost exclusively utilises poetry by Germanic authors for the texts and aside from two lieder, *The Long Furrow* (undated, text by A. Page)[147] and *Nobody* (c. 1988; text by J. Burger)[148], they are in entirely in German.

Although a portion of these lieder remain undated, the majority fall into two overarching creative periods which mirror his serious orchestral and chamber works. These are delineated into his 'Early Period' in which he was largely based in Vienna or Berlin (1915–33) and his 'Late Period' in New York City (1967–88). The majority of lieder in both periods are stylistically grounded in late Romanticism characteristic of Fin de siècle Vienna. One could point to composers such Franz Schreker, Alexander Zemlinsky, Joseph Marx, Richard Strauss, and Gustav Mahler as possible sources of influence while other selections show stylistic elements of composers such as Brahms and Schubert.

Lieder from the early period, comprised of nine works for voice and piano, begin in 1915 with a setting of Heinrich Heine's *Dämmernd liegt der Sommerabend* (c. 1915)[149] from his collection *Die Heimkehr* (1823–24). The relatively short piece (25 bars in ABA format) was composed before Burger's formal studies and is representative of his early lieder for voice and piano.[150] After a brief introduction in common time, marked allegretto grazioso, Burger utilises a gentle vocal line with light piano accompaniment to set the scene of the countryside in twilight (m. 1–11). A lively shift to C major opens the B section (m. 12–18) marked mezzo-forte. Burger utilised arpeggiated accompaniment in the piano allude to the rustling of brook, referenced which is the focal point of the text in the vocal line, before returning to the original A theme (m. 18) marked pianissimo.

This work in particular shares stylistic elements with that of Franz Schreker's earlier lieder works. Several other lieder with piano accompaniment follow on these stylings utilising Romantic poetry including *Regen* (8 November 1919, text by Johannes Schlaf)[151], *Seliges Ende* (17 November 1919, text

---

146 Julius Burger, *In dem Schatten meiner Locken* – a setting of the Hugo Wolf piece for voice and orchestra with text by Paul Heyse, EaZ-001-03-00526, Box 20, No. 1.2.4.2., Julius Burger (Bürger) Collection, Exilarte Zentrum Archiv der mdw, Vienna, Austria.

147 Julius Burger, *The Long Furrow*, lied for voice and piano with text by Anne Page, EaZ-001-03-00507, Box 17, No. 1.2.1.20., Julius Burger (Bürger) Collection, Exilarte Zentrum Archiv der mdw, Vienna, Austria.

148 Julius Burger, *Nobody* (1988), lied for voice and piano with text by Julius Burger, EaZ-001-03-00492 – 00494, Box 17, No. 1.2.1.16., Julius Burger (Bürger) Collection, Exilarte Zentrum Archiv der mdw, Vienna, Austria.

149 Julius Burger, *Dämmernd liegt der Sommerabend* (1915), lied for voice and piano with text by Heinrich Heine, EaZ-001-03-00467 – 00469, Box 17, No. 1.2.1.1., Julius Burger (Bürger) Collection, Exilarte Zentrum Archiv der mdw, Vienna, Austria.

150 Two formalised settings exist – one in G Major and the other in G flat Major. I utilised the setting in G flat for my evaluation.

151 Julius Burger, *Regen* (1919), lied for voice and piano with text by Johannes Schlaf, EaZ-001-03-00495 – 00496, Box 17, No. 1.2.1.2., Julius Burger (Bürger) Collection, Exilarte Zentrum Archiv der mdw, Vienna, Austria.

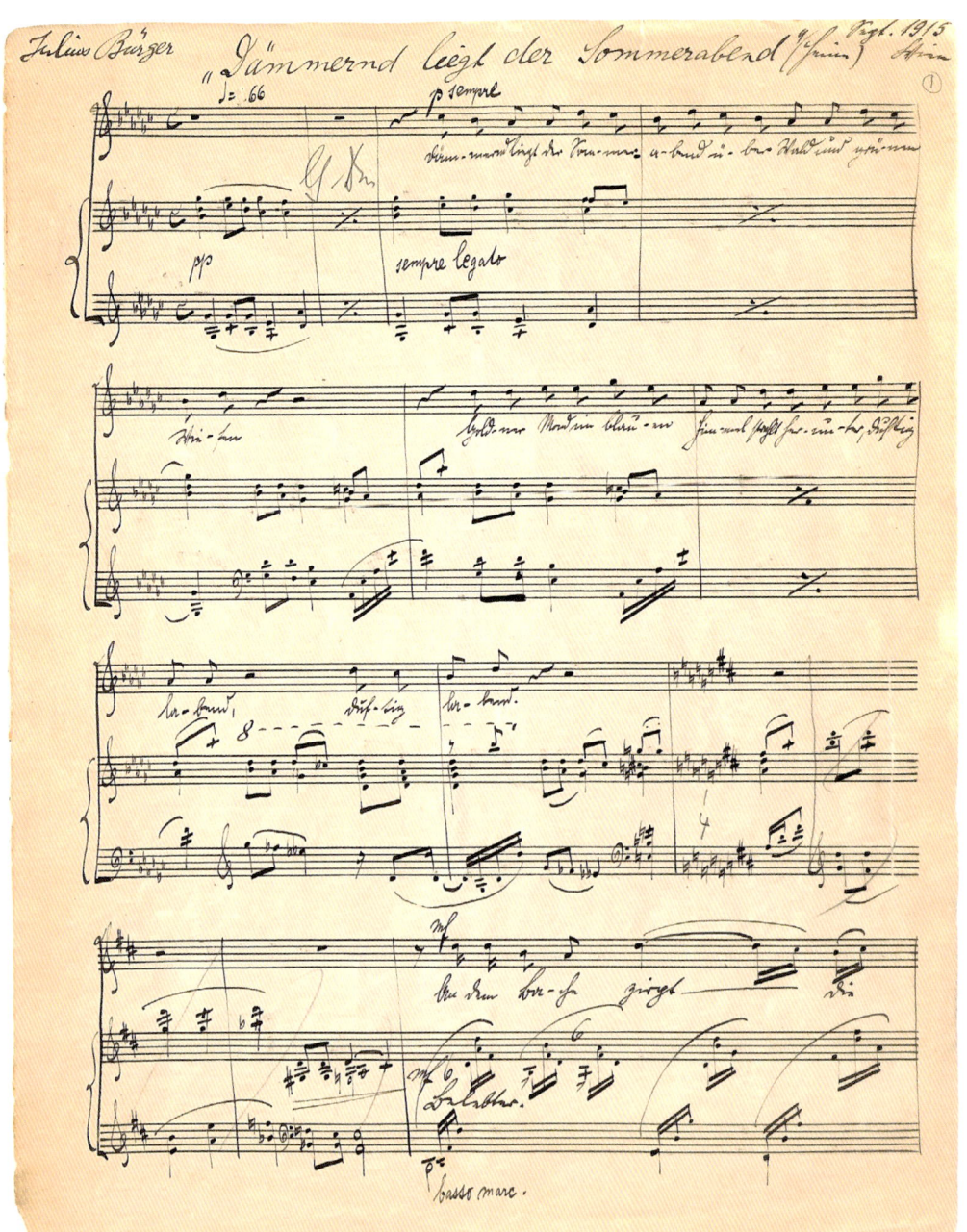

Burger's earliest known lied – *Dämmernd liegt der Sommerabend* (1915) – is a setting of poetry by Romantic poet Heinrich Heine. © A-Weaz

by F. K. Ginzkey)[152] , *Abendläuten* (19 January 1920, text by C. Morgenstern)[153] and *Lieder im Abend* (5 July 1926, text by H. von Meyerinck)[154]. The latter setting utilises a chromatic descend to represent Meyerinck's depiction of a tired hurdy gurdy man's song as it drifts over the countryside in the early summer evening. The piece opens in G major, marked lento and is written in 10/4 time. After a two-measure climatic build up in the accompaniment (m. 9–10) the vocal line returns in a climatic outburst utilising the characteristic chromaticism (m. 11–13) while the dynamics crescendo from mezzforte to fortissimo. The final four measures, marked piano, then slowly fade away as if drifting away with the warm summer breeze.

Four other lieder from this early period, addressed in the following 'Orchestral Lieder' section, align with Burger's preoccupation with larger orchestral forms in the 1920s and 30s. *Legende* (c. 1919, text by C. Morgenstern)[155] and the later lied *Stille der Nacht* (c. 1923, text by G. Keller)[156] are comparable to Mahler's orchestral lieder in their compositional style, libretti as well as the sheer size of the orchestral scoring. They were later paired together as a set titled *Two Songs for Baritone and Orchestra*. The other two orchestral lieder for tenor mark Burger's only commercial successes in his lifetime and are representative of lighter fare. These include the 'gypsy song' *Zigeunerlied* (recorded 1930) originally scored for a reduced orchestra and *Launisches Glück* (recorded 1932). Both were composed for, and subsequently recorded by, the famed Austro-Hungarian and Romanian tenor Joseph Schmidt.

While a definitive timeline cannot be completed due to handful of undated lieder, late 1967 marks the beginning of a major resurgence in compositional output for Burger. Despite a gap of over three decades, he seemingly picked up where he left off previously and produced four new lieder in the late Romantic musical idiom with text from Germanic poets. The pieces include *Dann* (c. 1967, text by Gottfried Benn)[157] in which Burger invokes Richard Strauss' lieder *Heimliche Aufforderung*, op. 27, no. 3 and *Traum durch die Dämmerung*,

---

152 Julius Burger, *Seliges Ende* (1919), lied for voice and piano with text by Franz Karl Ginzkey, EaZ-001-03-00500 – 00503, Box 17, No. 1.2.1.3., Julius Burger (Bürger) Collection, Exilarte Zentrum Archiv der mdw, Vienna, Austria.

153 Julius Burger, *Abendläuten* (1920), lied for voice and piano with text by Christian Morgenstern, EaZ-001-03-00458 – 00459, Box 17, No. 1.2.1.4., Julius Burger (Bürger) Collection, Exilarte Zentrum Archiv der mdw, Vienna, Austria.

154 Julius Burger, *Lieder im Abend* (1926), lied for voice and piano with text by Hubert von Meyerinck, EaZ-001-03-00487, Box 17, No. 1.2.1.5., Julius Burger (Bürger) Collection, Exilarte Zentrum Archiv der mdw, Vienna, Austria.

155 Julius Burger, *Legende* (1919), for baritone and orchestra with text by Christian Morgenstern, EaZ-001-03-00223 – 00230, Box 18, No. 1.2.3.2., Julius Burger (Bürger) Collection, Exilarte Zentrum Archiv der mdw, Vienna, Austria.

156 Julius Burger, *Stille der Nacht* (1923), for baritone and orchestra with text by Gottfried Keller, EaZ-001-03-00289 – 00350, Box 19, No. 1.2.3.3., Julius Burger (Bürger) Collection, Exilarte Zentrum Archiv der mdw, Vienna, Austria.

157 Julius Burger, *Dann* (1967), lied for voice and piano with text by Gottfried Benn, EaZ-001-03-00462 – 00465, Box 17, No. 1.2.1.7., Julius Burger, *Stille der Nacht* (1923), for baritone and orchestra with text by Gottfried Keller, EaZ-001-03-00289 – 00350, Box 19, No. 1.2.3.3., Julius Burger (Bürger) Collection, Exilarte Zentrum Archiv der mdw, Vienna, Austria.

op. 29, no. 1, *Auf ein Alte Partitur* (November 1967, text by Herbert Eulenberg)[158], *Liebesgedicht* (December 1967, text by Ricarda Huch)[159] and *Ein Winterabend* (31 December 1967, text by Georg Trakl).[160]

Two more followed in early 1968 including a setting of Klabund's *Man Soll in keiner Stadt* (1 January 1968)[161] and his shimmeringly beautiful treatment of A. von Halzfeld's *So Tanze, meine Seele vor dem Herrn!* (29 May 1968).[162] Burger's setting of Klabund's poem was likely chosen as a reflection of his own past experiences as an exile, drifting between Austria, Belgium, France, England and ending in the United States. Equally, it gives a positive, almost joyful treatment which is indicative, by many accounts, of his own demeanour and world outlook.

Lieder des Alters (No. 1.2.1.13.)

With the completion of his first song set in 1970, *Lieder des Alters* (c. 1970, 1975; various)[163], Burger takes a detour from the largely Romantic idiom of previous lieder and, in turn, this provides the set with a darker thematic undertone. The set consists of four lieder on text by Emmanuel Geibel (*Das ist das alte Lied und Leid* (1877)), Matthias Claudius (*Der Tod* (1798) and *Der Mensch* (1783)) and J. W. von Goethe (*Das Alter* (1783)). While the well-established texts aren't dramatically outside the typical realm from which Burger draws, his treatment is far more modern in which he seemingly flirts with the avant garde and tonally ambiguous practices more akin to modernist music of the Second Viennese School. The reoccurring literary themes of this collection are a contemplation on the trials of life, old age, and death.

The collection commences with *Das ist das alte Lied und Leid* (E. Geibel) in a *Langsam* tempo and is atonal throughout. It moves between a succession of major and minor keys (C minor, E flat minor, E Major, F Major). Burger creates a dark

---

158 Julius Burger, *Auf eine alte Partitur* (1967), lied for voice and piano with text by Herbert Eulenberg, EaZ-001-03-00460, Box 17, No. 1.2.1.9., Julius Burger, *Stille der Nacht* (1923), for baritone and orchestra with text by Gottfried Keller, EaZ-001-03-00289 – 00350, Box 19, No. 1.2.3.3., Julius Burger (Bürger) Collection, Exilarte Zentrum Archiv der mdw, Vienna, Austria.

159 Julius Burger, *Liebesgedicht* (1967), lied for voice and piano with text by Ricarda Huch, EaZ-001-03-00479, Box 17, No. 1.2.1.8., Julius Burger, *Stille der Nacht* (1923), for baritone and orchestra with text by Gottfried Keller, EaZ-001-03-00289 – 00350, Box 19, No. 1.2.3.3., Julius Burger (Bürger) Collection, Exilarte Zentrum Archiv der mdw, Vienna, Austria.

160 Julius Burger, *Winterabend* (1967), lied for voice and piano with text by Georg Trakl, EaZ-001-03-00470 – 00472, Box 17, No. 1.2.1.6., Julius Burger, *Stille der Nacht* (1923), for baritone and orchestra with text by Gottfried Keller, EaZ-001-03-00289 – 00350, Box 19, No. 1.2.3.3., Julius Burger (Bürger) Collection, Exilarte Zentrum Archiv der mdw, Vienna, Austria.

161 Julius Burger, *Man soll in keiner Stadt …* (1968), lied for voice and piano with text by Klabund (Alfred Henschke), EaZ-001-03-00488 – 00490, Box 17, No. 1.2.1.10., Julius Burger (Bürger) Collection, Exilarte Zentrum Archiv der mdw, Vienna, Austria.

162 Julius Burger, *So tanze meine Seele, vor dem Herrn!* (1968), lied for voice and piano with text by Adolf von Hatzfeld, EaZ-001-03-00504 – 00506, Box 17, No. 1.2.1.11., Julius Burger (Bürger) Collection, Exilarte Zentrum Archiv der mdw, Vienna, Austria.

163 Julius Burger, *Lieder des Alters* (1970), lieder setting of four pieces for voice and piano with texts by Geibel, Claudius, von Goethe, EaZ-001-03-00480 – 00486, Box 17, No. 1.2.1.13., Julius Burger (Bürger) Collection, Exilarte Zentrum Archiv der mdw, Vienna, Austria.

Examples from Burger's experimental song cycle *Lieder des Alters* (1970; 1975). © A-Weaz

atmosphere from the very beginning by utilising harmonically disjointed chords in the accompaniment. When combined with the tempo marking, these chords evoke a sense of time passing or possibly death knells which, in turn, sets the mood for the work. This emotive idea is present in the accompaniment in one form or another throughout this collection. The first selection is largely marked piano and punctuated only by short forte 'outbursts' ("*verrauchen*" m. 9–10; "... *Kunst, das Leben recht zu brauchen*" m. 27–9) before dissipating.

The second lied *Der Tod* (M. Claudius) is surprisingly brief. Marked '*Largo*' in B-flat minor, Burger utilises a Basso ostinato progression in octaves (B-flat, G-flat, F, C) in the bass accompaniment throughout the piece. This is a continuation of the passing time motif and is further supported in the final phrase which makes reference to a clock striking the hour ("... *und die Stunde schlägt*" m.13–15). The dynamic markings for the piece do not rise above a 'piano' marking as if to evoke hushed tones of mourners in a crypt ("*Ach, es ist so dunkel in des Todes Kammer...*" m. 3–5). It is possible Burger drew inspiration for this lied from Schubert's *Der Doppelgänger* from his cycle Schwanengesang, D. 957 for the use of a Basso ostinato, dynamics and setting in minor key.

Der Mensch, also with text by Claudius, is the most tonally grounded of the collection in G minor, despite the key signature. The lied follows a similar tempo marking of *Adagio* and is in common time. In keeping with the overarching literary themes, the poetry is set utilising straightforward voice leading in a dynamically subdued tone. Only in the final third of the piece (m. 28 onward) does Burger utilise a dynamic marking louder than *Mezzo forte*. In the final section, marked *Grave*, he reintroduces the vocal line from the piece's first phrase (m. 2–6) in which the text describes the birth of the 'Mensch' ("*Empfangen und genähret vom Weibe wunderbar...*") to provide a full circle of life with the same music marking the end of life ("*Und alles dieses währet, wenn's hoch kommt, achzig Jahr...*"; m. 28–33). Burger then reiterates the final line of the text three times. He makes use of an a cappella line to great effect and with each reiteration of the final line of text ("*nimmer wieder...*") the piece diminishes dynamically as the accompaniment concludes, marked pianississimo.

In contrast with the other works in this collection, the final lied, titled *Das Alter*, is almost playful and is more free in tonality. It continues the ticking effect, albeit in a lively *allegretto grazioso* tempo, to symbolise the perception of time passing faster as one ages. This first collection of songs, much like his string quartets no. 2 and 3, are not typical of Burger's compositional style grounded in late Romanticism of the early twentieth century but show his ability to successfully experiment outside his own comfort zone.

Vier Heitere Lieder (No. 1.2.1.14.)

Nine years after the completion of his first lieder set, *Lieder des Alters*, Burger composed a second lieder collection utilising selections of poetry from *Kleinigkeiten* (1751, Frankfurt & Leipzig) by eighteenth-century German playwright Gotthold Ephraim Lessing's (1729–1781). This collection, titled *Vier Heitere Lieder* (1979; various)[164], is thematically and musical-

---

164 Julius Burger, *Vier Heitere Lieder* (1979), lieder setting of four pieces for voice and piano with texts by Gotthold Ephraim Lessing, EaZ-001-03-00515 – 00523, Box 17, No. 1.2.1.14., Julius Burger (Bürger) Collection, Exilarte Zentrum Archiv der mdw, Vienna, Austria.

ly removed from Burger's first lieder set and instead focuses on the cheerful subjects of love and wine. It is also a return to the idiomatic vein of late Romanticism present in most of his other lieder.

The first piece, *Der Irrtum*, utilises waltz-like *allegretto* in F Major to kick off the 'tongue in cheek' collection. The text is written from the point of view of a passer-by on a busy city street. A scantily clad woman named Lotte peers down from her upper floor window, dog in tow, attempting to gain the attention of those below (m. 4–29). The accompaniment, marked *meno mosso* (m. 31) then broadens (key of F minor) to emphasise the 'innocent' nature of the narrator as, lost in thought, he stares up at Lotte (m. 31–6). The original playful tempo is quickly regained (A flat Major) as Lotte smiles roguishly at her apparent onlooker (m. 39–53) before the piece returns with the broader 'innocent' declarations of the narrator marked *forte* (m. 54–62). The punchline is then revealed in a return to the original tempo (m. 64) as the narrator professes it was her colourful dog he was looking at rather than Lotte ("*Ich sah nach ihrem bunten Hunde, es ist ein artig tier*", m. 64–83). As with the final line of each of the poem's three stanzas, Burger re-emphasises for effect. The first lied concludes in F Major with a cheeky and playful coda, marked *presto*, which emphasises the jovial nature of the collection.

The second lied in the collection, *Die Nahmen*, adopts a subtler tone from the antics in the first. This love song follows on the premise of Shakespeare's famed line from Romeo and Juliet "*What's in a name? / That which we call a rose / By any other name would smell as sweet.*"[165] The piece commences with a gentle, expressive G Major introduction in the accompaniment, marked *Andante*. Burger then commences the vocal line ("*Ich fragte meine Schöne...*", m. 4–6) with a nod to the opening vocal phrase of Franz Schubert's *Der Neugierige* op. 25, no. 6 ("*Ich fragte keine Blume...*", m. 4–6). Burger then sets forward creating an undulating line for the vocalist over light accompaniment as the text states "*What name shall I call you in my song? ("Wie soll mein Lied dich nennen?"*, m. 6–8). The question is immediately followed with a succession of goddesses from Greek mythology (m. 8–14) before the story recollects on the lover's response ("*Ach! Namen sind nur Töne*", m.18–24). For the vocal phrase (m. 27–30), Burger then reiterates the music from the original question (m. 10–16). After a brief modulation to B flat Major in the accompaniment, Burger returns with a sensual line "*Nur nenne mich die Deine*" ("*Only, call me yours!*", m. 32-7), ending the lied in G Major.

The collection then returns to the playful, tongue in cheek antics in the third installment, *Die Schöne von Hinten*. The text is from the point of view of two youths who have spotted what appears to be a beautiful woman from behind. After getting his friend's attention ("*Sieh Freund! Sie da!*", m. 4-5) the first youth begins to list the beautiful attributes of the woman from her modern dress, tidy walk, and neck full of dark curls to her slender body (m. 11–20). Burger opens this piece in a '*tempo di marcia*' in F Major and gives the impression foot traffic on a busy city street by utilising left hand quaver passages in the accompaniment. The motif is frequently staccato which punctuates and emotes a perception of the youths 'sneaking' to catch a glimpse of the woman. Burger then increases the intensity ever so slightly with an *accelerando* in the accompaniment into m. 24, marked *Piu mosso* in A-flat major. After a short interlude featuring the 'sneaky' staccato motif (m. 24–

---

165 William Shakespeare, *Romeo and Juliet*, Act II, scene II, Line 47-48. First published in 1597.

Title page to 'Die Küsse' – the concluding piece to Burger's 'tongue-in-cheek' collection *Vier Heitere Lieder* (1979). © A-Weaz

Right: The sumptuous finale of 'Die Küsse' which extols the kisses from lover Cynthia "Ja! Das ist ein Kuss!" © A-Weaz

7) the youth intensify their mission in order to gain a closer look and even exclaim she must be like the goddesses Venus or Phyllis ("*Es muss, trügt nicht der hint're Schein, Die Venus oder Phyllis sein*", m. 32–6).

This whips the youths into a frenzy as the woman begins to turn in their direction. Burger steps the vocal line up chromatically to bring the chase to a climatic point ("*Jetzt sieht sie ungefähr zurücke*", m. 41–3) only for the youths to discover, disappointedly, she is an old woman in stylish clothes ("*Was war's, das mich entzückt gemacht? Ein altes Weib in junger Tracht!*", m. 43). Burger leaves room for the vocalist to deliver this phrase *ad libitum*. He then moves the accompaniment through a series of key changes in quick succession to emote a musical representation of the old woman in G minor (m. 44–8) before returning to the key of F major as the vocal line proclaims "*Ein altes Weib in junger Tracht!*" ("An old woman in youthful clothes!", m. 49–50).

The concluding piece, titled *Die Küsse*, is an impressive centrepiece to the set. The thematic subject focuses on the many different types of kisses and their meanings. The piece, marked *allegretto*, commences with a playful chromatic piano theme in the accompaniment that reoccurs throughout the piece. The first verse in F Major (m.1–9) focuses on the kisses of a child, which are innocent and are only for fun. Burger highlights the lively spirit of a child by marking the majority of the vocal line with a staccato accent while emphasising key words with tenuto markings ("*... nur noch spielt*", m. 3; "*... den man nicht fühlt*", m. 8–9).

The piece then moves onto descriptions of receiving kisses upon meeting a friend with rolled chords under the vocal line in F minor. This section emotes a decidedly formal, if not cold, feeling (m. 10–14) but quickly moves onto a familiar state as the text addresses a kiss of blessing bestowed on his son. This 'father' section (m. 14–21) is in A flat Major. Burger first utilises half note chordal progressions in the accompaniment (m. 15–16) to instil a sense of authority, respect, and broadness of a paternal figure.

The following section, marked Allegro, returns in E major with the playful triplet figure motif from the first section to usher in a lively address of a kiss from a sister (m. 22–30). Burger utilises this section to broaden the accompaniment part in anticipation for the final climatic section. The final phrase of the 'sister' section ("*An andre Mädchen denken kann*", m. 28–30) gives way as the grand finale is ushered in with a large crescendo and accelerated cascading effect in the accompaniment (m. 30).

Burger unfurls a sumptuous concluding section in A Major while illuminating the proclamations in the text of Cynthia's kiss (m. 30–36). After modulating back into F Major (via D minor; m.36-7), the accompaniment makes a playful call and response with the vocal line by once again utilising the triplet figure motif. The point is driven home as Burger reiterates the phrase "*Ja so ein Kuss*" before giving the vocal line a dramatic last phrase "*Das ist ein Kuss!*" (m. 42) ending on a high F as the accompaniment concludes with oscillating triplet chords and ends on a rolled F major chord.

Burger's jovial personality shines through with this masterfully nuanced collection. There is evidence to suggest Burger thought the *Vier Heitere Lieder* may be a successful addition to the classical concert scene and forwarded a copy to famed

German lieder interpreter, baritone Dietrich Fischer-Dieskau in 1981.[166] Evidence suggests he later made inquiries into having this collection published with Musikverlag Cranz, who printed a vocal and piano version of his early success *Launisches Glück*.[167] Whilst it was well received with both parties, the *Vier Heitere Lieder* collection remains unpublished.

Late lieder

Several other notable lieder should be mentioned as they seem to represent Burger's personal reflections on his experiences as an émigré. Although a manuscript of his lied *Der Wiener liebt Amerika* is not present in the Burger collection of the Exilarte Archiv, the title is among a comprehensive list of compositions in a personal notebook of the composer.[168] If taken at face value, the title appears to be a musical love letter to his adopted country, although this is not discernible without locating a surviving copy. His final two lieder provide a bookend to an œuvre spanning 73 years.

Nobody[169] and *Goodbye, Vienna*,[170] both composed in 1988, are unique for several reasons. Both pieces are settings of original texts by the composer and thus, are the only two works in his entire repertoire which share this unique quality. Despite their titles, only *Nobody* contains English text while *Goodbye, Vienna* (also referred to as the *Wienerlied*) contains original text in German. The former piece in G major is brisk, with pitter-patter style and sparse accompaniment. The simple form and text gives the piece a musical theatre quality. The text exclaims "*Nobody is a Nobody, Ev'rebody is a Somebody*" (m. 2–5) and continues to assure that lucky, chance occurrences happen all the time, and everywhere (m. 6–19). The piece concludes with a repeated affirmation "*He's a fool who does not believe, ... that ev'ry body is a somebody!*" (m. 29–35).

Burger's final composition, *Goodbye, Vienna*, brings Burger's œuvre back to the cultural traditions of his native Austria with a personal homage to the Wienerlied genre. Burger's melancholic swan song reflects on the happy days of his youth while contemplating the now long past world in which he inhabited. The introduction in C major set the tone "*Einmal lebte ich in Wien, im schönen Wien. Aber Jetzt ist es nicht mehr mein Wien*" ("*Once I lived in Vienna, in beautiful Vienna. But now it is no more my Vienna*", m. 3–11) before entering the body of the Wienerlied with a modulation to C minor (m. 12). The piece then begins to pick up pace (m. 21)

---

166 Office of Dietrich Fischer-Dieskau, "Letter to Julius Burger," 30 November 1981, Julius Burger Collection, Exilarte Zentrum Archiv der mdw, Vienna, Austria.

167 Julius Burger, "Letter to Herr Nietzel- Musikverlag Cranz," 11 October 1989, Julius Bürger Collection, Exilarte Zentrum Archiv der mdw, Vienna, Austria.

168 Source: Julius Burger, "Composition list," from personal papers held in the private collection of Dr. Trude Zörer, Vienna, Austria.

169 Julius Burger, *Nobody* (1988), lied for voice and piano with text by Julius Burger, EaZ-001-03-00492 – 00494, Box 17, No. 1.2.1.16., Julius Burger (Bürger) Collection, Exilarte Zentrum Archiv der mdw, Vienna, Austria.

170 Julius Burger, *Goodbye, Vienna* (1988), lied for voice and piano with text by Julius Burger, EaZ-001-03-00474 – 00476; 00581, Box 17, No. 1.2.1.17., Julius Burger, *Nobody* (1988), lied for voice and piano with text by Julius Burger, EaZ-001-03-00492 – 00494, Box 17, No. 1.2.1.16., Julius Burger (Bürger) Collection, Exilarte Zentrum Archiv der mdw, Vienna, Austria.

One of only two known lieder in English, *Nobody* (1988) utilises original text by Burger in a pitter-patter like tempo. © A-Weaz

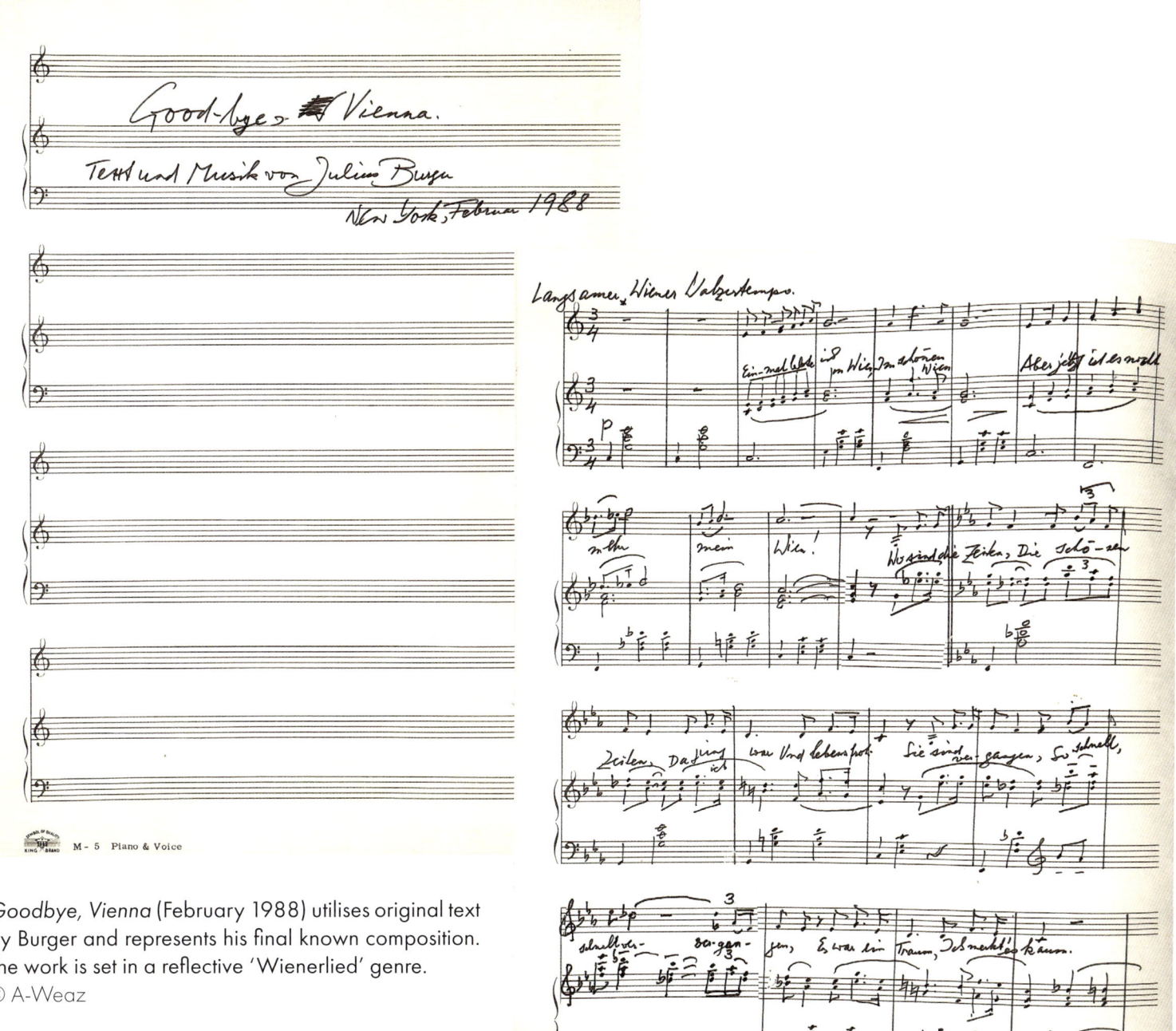

Goodbye, Vienna (February 1988) utilises original text by Burger and represents his final known composition. The work is set in a reflective 'Wienerlied' genre.
© A-Weaz

before the climatic phrase "*Das Glück in seiner Hand, weiss nicht wie es entschwand*" is immediately followed by a characteristically dramatic pause (m. 25–7). The piece then returns to the original tempo with the text ruminating on the original question "*Wo sind die Zeiten, die schönen Zeiten?*" before concluding "*Sie sind vorbei, So schnell vorbei!*" ("*Where are those times, those joyful times? They are gone, so quickly gone!*" (m. 27–32).

3.2.2 Voice and Orchestra (Catalogue 1.2.3.)

Given Burger's strengths as a composer and arranger for the medium of orchestra, it isn't a surprise to find inclusions of original orchestral lieder as well as vocal and piano lieder arranged for orchestral accompaniment. In total, nine works for the medium exist. The first four, *Legende* (1919), *Stille der Nacht* (1923), *Zigeunerlied* (1929–30) and *Launisches Glück* (1932) stem from his early period in Vienna and Berlin (1915–1933). The remaining five works stem from his lengthy New York City period (1939–1988). These consist of arrangements of his own lieder (*So Tanze mein Seele*, 29 May 1968; *Venedig*, November 1970; and *Schlummerlied*, undated) as well as two orchestrated arrangements of lieder by Hugo Wolf: *Verborgenheit* (*Mörike Lieder*, no. 12) and *In dem Schatten meiner Locken* (*Spanisches Liederbuch*, no. 2). The previous three arrangements stem from early 1985[171] while the orchestrated Wolf lieder, although undated, most likely stem from the early New York period as apparent from the CBS manuscript paper on which they were written.[172]

Two Songs for Baritone and Orchestra: Legende (1919) and Stille der Nacht (1923)

These two works, which were later paired together as a set, represent Burger's first segue into late Romantic form most widely associated with early twentieth century Germany and Austria among the likes of Gustav Mahler, Richard Strauss, Zemlinsky, Max Reger and Joseph Marx.

Legende (Box 18, No. 1.2.3.2.) is a sectional work for baritone and enhanced orchestra. Burger created a dark, operatic atmosphere through his musical setting of a poem from German poet Christian Morgenstern's (1871–1914) *Christzyklus*. The poem portrays Jesus Christ who, whilst walking toward Gethsemane to pray at the Mount of Olives, comes across a party of peasants dancing. The work is comprised of several sections and throughout Burger draws on his aptitude for storytelling by utilising a wide palette of timbres, dynamics and specific instrumentation in the orchestra to illuminate the poetry. One example of his skills in this area is the reoccurring use of a three-note motif which first comes out prominently in the *andante* section (m. 36). It is used to symbolise the main character trudging through the countryside and again to represent the dancing at the party via the rhythmic strumming of cellos at the *allegretto* section (m. 70). Burger also includes a solo tune for oboe to represent the reedy music of a peasant's bagpipe (m. 72). The three-note motif then returns in the concluding section on timpani (m. 200-8). The final iteration could possibly symbolise death knells as Christ continues his fateful journey.

171 See manuscripts
172 See manuscripts

Burger's knowledge of the vocal capabilities for the baritone fach are also readily apparent through his carefully crafted vocal leading. Equally, he uses the unaccompanied vocal line to great effect in order to highlight the drama of the text. A poignant example is at the piece's dramatic climax (m. 145) where the baritone sings "*Da brach auf eines Jüngers Wink des Spielers Weise jählings ab – ein krampfhaft Zucken überschrack des Meisters hagre Hochgestalt*" ("*Then, at a nod from one disciple, the player's tune stopped abruptly – a convulsive tremor shot through the Master's tall, gaunt figure*").

Stille der Nacht (Box 19, No. 1.2.3.3.) also requires an enhanced orchestra characteristic of late-nineteenth and early-twentieth century orchestral lieder by the likes of Gustav Mahler (1860–1911). *Stille der Nacht* was composed by Burger whilst he was employed at the opera house in Karlsruhe, Germany in 1923.[173] For the text, Burger turned to a poem by German-Swiss writer Gottfried Keller (1819–1890), arguably the leading nineteenth-century figure of "poetic realism" (*Poetischer Realismus*).[174] Keller's poem 'Nacht, No. 5'[175] ('Stille der Nacht') has its poetic emphasis on the beauty and wonder of nature. This is a central theme of *Romantik* poetry. Like *Legende*, *Stille der Nacht* shows Burger's attention to the demands of the vocal line while providing the baritone soloist with soaring, lyrical phrases.

Burger's exquisite setting evokes Keller's descriptions of the night sky, opening with an ethereal flute solo (marked *adagio*) in the introduction. Burger heightens the ethereal quality by supplementing the score with harp, celeste, piano as well as organ and bells. The undulating motif (m. 21–81) of *Stille der Nacht* appears early in the piece and is scored for English horns, muted trumpets and trombones. This motif later reappears in the strings (m. 129), followed in the brass and flutes (m. 133) and shortly after in the woodwinds (m. 135) and timpani (m. 137). The reintroduced motif gives way to the lied's rapturous climax as the baritone soloist sings his final, exalted declaration "*Der letzte leise Schmerz und Spott...*" (m. 141–57). The final stanza is concluded with the full orchestra and cymbal clashes (m. 156–70). It then begins to recede leaving the strings ascending in chromatic tremolos interspersed with woodwinds, harp celeste and the piano. The oboe returns for a final reiteration of the ethereal motif (m. 179–83) first introduced by the flute. Sustained horns set a base as the celeste and piano make their final interjections as the strings utilise a soft, sustained flageolet effect (m. 186–9) which falls away to silence.

When paired with *Legende*, the two works form an impressive set deemed *Two Songs for Baritone and Orchestra*.[176]

---

173 Julius Burger, "Composition list," from personal papers held in the private collection of Dr. Trude Zörer, Vienna, Austria, p.44.

174 Britannica, T. Editors of Encyclopaedia. "Gottfried Keller." *Encyclopedia Britannica*, July 15, 2021. https://www.britannica.com/biography/Gottfried-Keller, Accessed 21 January 2022.

175 Gottfried Keller, "Nacht, No.5," from *Gedichte* (*Natur*), (Heidelberg: Verlag Carl Winter, 1846).

176 Two Songs for Baritone and Orchestra was first premiered by Austrian baritone Michael Kraus as part of the *Konzert mit Werken von Julius Bürger* in Berlin's Jesus Christus Kirche in Berlin on 29 September 1994. The concert also featured Burger's *Scherzo für Orchester, Konzert für Violoncello und Orchester* with American cellist Maya Beiser as well as his *Variationen über ein Thema von Carl Philipp Emanuel Bach*. The pieces were performed by the Berlin Radio Symphony Orchestra under the direction of Australian conductor Simone Young. Source: Julius Burger, "Konzert mit Werken von Julius Bürger," Stagebill, Rundfunk-Sinfonieorchester Berlin, Maya Beiser, cello, Michael Kraus, baritone, cond. Simone Young, Jesus Christus Kirche, Berlin, 29 September 1994.

Legende (1919) is one of two orchestral lieder which comprise Burger's Two Songs for Baritone and Orchestra. The second photo shows Burger's theatrical use of a cappella to great effect. © A-Weaz

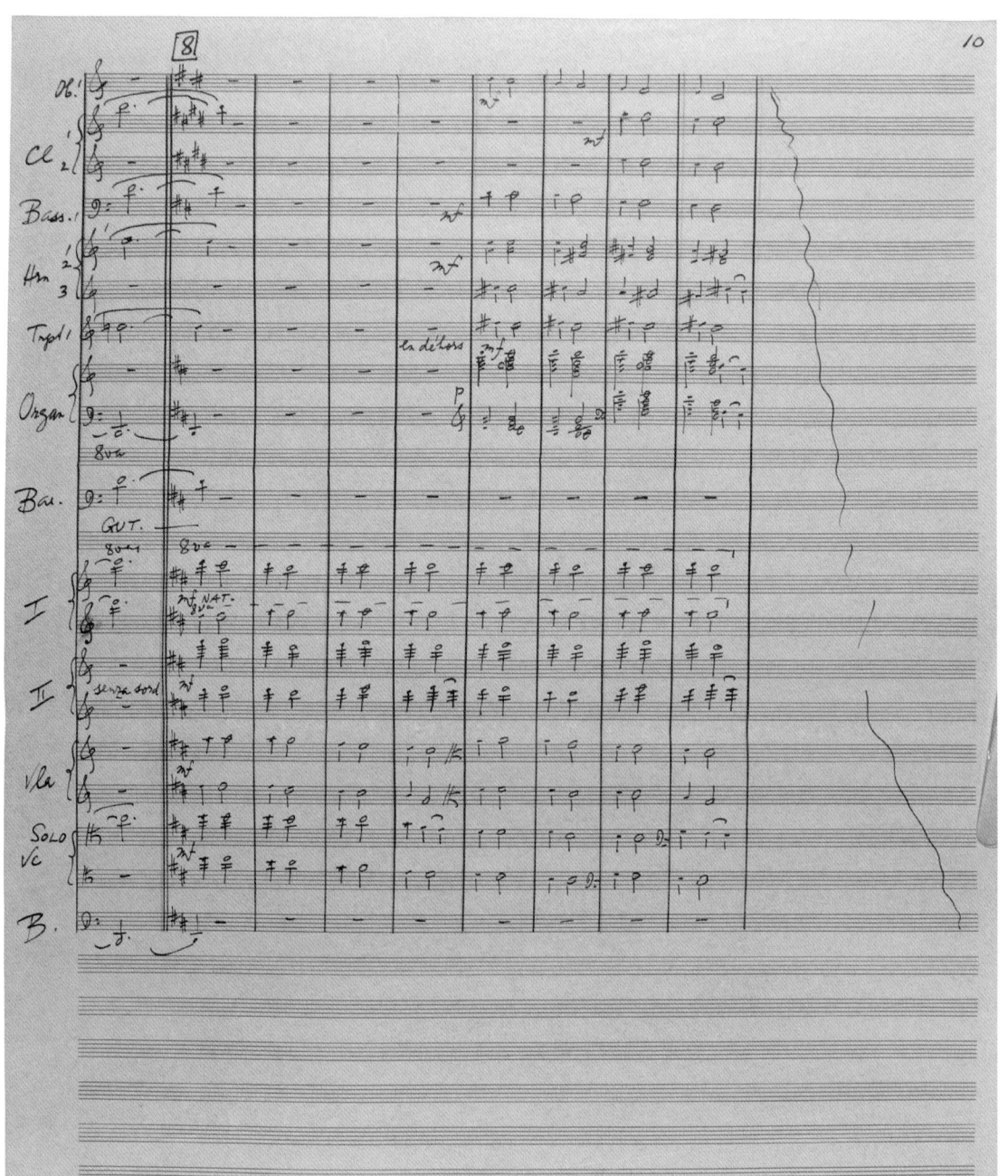

This illustration, from Burger's ethereal work of beauty *Stille der Nacht* (1923), highlights the orchestral cascading effect into the climax. © A-Weaz

DER LETZ-TE, LEI-SE SCHMERZ UND SPOTT VER- SCHWIN- DET

Zigeunerlied (1929–30) and *Launisches Glück* (1932)

As previously noted, these two works represent the only commercial successes of Burger's compositional career. Both were written for and recorded by the Austro-Hungarian / Romanian tenor Joseph Schmidt. *Zigeunerlied* was composed for Schmidt in late 1929 and was recorded by the singer, accompanied by conductor Lajos Kiss and his light 'Gypsy' orchestra on the Ultraphon/Telefunken label in February 1930.[177] It is apparent Burger found this work had continued appeal and later reworked it into a chamber piece for violin with piano accompaniment (*Zigeunerlied* for violin and piano; Box 6–7, No, 1.1.3.1.2.4.–1.1.3.1.2.11). It was then reworked a third time for violin and orchestral accompaniment (*Zigeunerlied* for violin and orchestra; Box 6 - 7, 1.1.3.1.2.1. - 3.; 1.1.3.1.2.12. - 15.). While the two arrangements are included in the archival documentation of Exilarte, his original work for voice and light accompaniment is lost. Equally, Burger did attempt to promote the violin and piano version with the BBC in early 1930s but the violin part was considered too difficult for the players of the music department.[178] Both arranged versions for violin were later premiered in the revival concerts in the 1990s.[179]

The work is stylistically of the Austro-Hungarian folk tradition with particular emphasis on the music of the Roma people. In an examination of the Schmidt recording and the violin and piano arrangement, the work opens in solemn *lento* in G minor with the song (Schmidt version) portraying a poor gypsy youth who pleads with his love to reject the advances of a rich suitor and stay with him ("*Dich nur, mein Glück – mit nassen Augen fleh ich, ach kehr zurück!*"). The work, in two sections, takes a decisively different tone in the latter half with a lively allegro tempo as the man's love turns from passionate attempts to regain his love ("*Komm und küss mich, komm und lieb' mich...*") to scorn and vengeance against both the suitor and lover ("*Ei das Hochzeitslied spiel ich selber, wenn die Geige schluchzend schreit, töt ich dich und ihn, Hei!*").[180] The original version of *Zigeunerlied* features an impressive line for the violin which undoubtedly gave Burger the idea for an expanded violin and piano version and, later, the violin and orchestral arrangement.

Launisches Glück, also composed for Joseph Schmidt, is a beautifully lyric lied full of late Romantic Viennese schmaltz. Burger's version, with lyrics by Leopold Hainisch, utilised thematic material derived from Johann Strauss Jr's lied "O

---

177 Alfred A. Fassbind, *Joseph Schmidt: Sein Lied ging um die Welt*, (Zürich: Römerhof Verlag, 2012),p.299.

178 Stanford Robinson, "Letter to Julius Burger re: Zigeunerlied," 21 December 1934, From Burger, Julius. 31-42. R27/40/2. BBC Music-General: Burger, Julius. BBC Written Archives Centre, Reading, England.

179 *Zigeunerlied* for Violin and Piano was first performed on 1 May 1991 at a chamber concert of Julius Burger's music held by the America-Israeli Cultural Foundation in New York City; *Zigeunerlied* for Violin and Orchestra was first performed in an orchestral concert of Julius Burger's works at Alice Tully Hall in New York City on 3 June 1991 by the Orchestra of St. Luke's conducted by Paul Lustig Dunkel with violin solo performed by Sergiu Schwartz. Source: "The Orchestra of St. Luke's perform the works of Julius Burger," Lincoln Center Stagebill, June 1991, p.13-16B, 33.

180 Joseph Schmidt "Zigeunerlied" by Julius Bürger, Lajos Kiss and his Zigeunerorchestra, Recorded 12 February 1930, 30422, Germany: Ultraphon / Telefunken E 373, Austria: Kalliope K 702, Shellac 78rpm.

schöner Mai" (*Prinz Methusalem*, 1877)[181] coupled with his own ideas to create this commercial success. The lied was also incorporated into the Strauss operetta *1,001 Nights* in which Schmidt featured. The orchestral version was recorded by Parlophon Berlin and featured Schmidt and the Staatskapelle Orchestra Berlin conducted by Dr. Weissmann.[182] While the original manuscript is not among the Burger collection in Exilarte, a vocal and piano arrangement was published by Musikverlag Cranz in 1932.[183] Since its publication, the piece has been recorded multiple times between 1932 and 1960.[184]

3.2.3 Choral Works (Catalogue 1.2.5.)

Among Burger's large collection of vocal works are four known choral compositions on Christian and Jewish religious themes. These titles include *The Final Amen, Hallelujah* (Box 22, No. 1.2.5.1.3.), *Miserere* (Box 20–21, No. 1.2.5.1.2.) and *Service for the Sabbath Morning* for cantor, mixed choir, and organ (Box 20, No. 1.2.5.1.1.). Additionally, Burger's choral works include an arrangement of Johann Strauss Jr's renown waltz *An der Schönen Blauen Donau* for two pianos, four soli and chorus.[185] The location of this work, however, is unknown. Of these compositions, only one has a composition date. *Miserere* utilises a poem by Austrian novelist and poet Ferdinand von Saar (1833–1906) set for choir and organ and was completed while Burger was still a student of the Vienna academy in 1917.[186] It is also the only one of his choral works which has been publicly performed to date.[187]

181 Strauss later recycled some of the thematic material from the lied to create a waltz by the same title, op.375.

182 Alfred A. Fassbind, *Joseph Schmidt: Sein Lied ging um die Welt*, (Zürich: Römerhof Verlag, 2012), p.290.

183 Julius Burger, "Launisches Glück: Lied nach Motiven von Joh. Strauss," Text by L. Hainisch, Klavier arr. By von Michaeloff, C. 47427a, Bruxelles: Musikverlag Cranz, 1932.

184 *Launisches Glück* has been recorded commercially numerous times by singers such as Joseph Schmidt (1904-1942): recorded 18 February 1932, 133438: Germany - B.48154, 133438-3, Germany- Parlophon B. 48154 / Odeon 0-25982, England - Parlophone R 1330, Australia - R 3550, America- Decca P-20311; Karl Jöken (1893-1971): Kristall 6084 – Matr.MC 2122 (1932); Charles Kullmann (1903–1983): Columbia DW 3046 – Matrix WR 406 (1932); Friedrich Eugen Engels (1909–1994): Polydor 10999 – Matr. 7943 ½ GR 3 (1933); Leonardo Aramesco (1898–1946) : Grammophon 1263 – Matr. 5095 BD8 (1933); Rudolf Schock (1915–1986) : Electrola – E21 642 / Electrola – 45-EG 9129 (1960).

185 This work is included in the composition list in his personal papers with Lyrics by Ruth Martin.
Source: Julius Burger, "Composition list", from personal papers held in the private collection of Dr. Trude Zörer, Vienna, Austria, p.76

186 Other composers who have set works by von Saar include Franz Liszt's lied *Des Tages laute Stimmen schweigen*, S.337 (1880) as well as two by Burger's former teacher, Franz Schreker including the lied *Stimmen des Tages* (*Zwei Gesänge* Op.2, No.2 (1901)) as well as the choral setting of *Gesang der Armen in Winter* (1902) for a cappella mixed chorus, among others.

187 Premiered 20 February 1993 by the New York Virtuosos Singers under the direction of Harold Rosenbaum at St Peter's Church in New York City. A second performance of the work was given at the Cathedral of St. John the Divine as part of a concert by the New Orchestra of Westchester on in October 1993. Source: "An Evening of Premieres," *New York Times*, 19 February 1993, C17, p.63.

Miserere – using text by Ferdinand von Saar – was first premiered in concert on 20 February 1993 at St. Peter's Church, NYC. © A-Weaz

Cover of the parlour arrangement for Burger's *Launisches Glück* (1932). Cranz Publishing, Brussels. 1932.
© Zentralbibliotek Zürich

In contrast to the other vocal works in German and English, Burger's cantorial work for choir and organ utilise text in transliterated Hebrew. The untitled work utilising passages from the Torah as well as blessings which are regularly used in religious observance practices and was written for a Jewish Shabbat service. The work is in seventeen sections titled as follows: I. *Mah town* (Ma Tova – prayer on entering Temple), II. *Bor'chu es Adonoy* (Blessing before opening the Torah), III. *Sh'mah*, IV. *Mi chomocho* (Mi Khamokha – reference to daily prayers), V. *Tzur Yisroel* (Psalms 19:5), VI. *Kedusha* (several prayers recited – commonly Isaiah 6:3, Ezekiel 3:12, Psalms 146:10), VII. *May the Words* (Psalms 19:14), VIII. *S'u sh'orim* (Psalms 24), IX. *Baruch shenosan toroh* (Blessed be the Torah), X and XI. *Sh'ma Yisroel* (in two parts), XII. *L'cho Adonoy, Gad'lu*, XIII. *Hodo al eretz*, XIV. *Ez chayim* (*Etz hayim hi* or Tree of Life – Proverbs 3:18), XV. *Waanachnu* (Va'anahnu – Psalms 20), XVI. *On that day* and concludes with the hymn XVII. *En kelohenu* (*Ein Keloheinu*).

Many prominent composers of Burger's era wrote their own Jewish liturgical music or utilised elements in their compositions. Examples include Ernest Bloch's work *Advodat Hakodesh* for baritone, chorus and orchestra (c.1930–33)[188] as well as the multiple incorporations by Arnold Schoenberg (*Kol Nidre*, op. 39; *Die Jakobsleiter*, *A Survivor from Warsaw* which utilises the prayer *Shema Yisrael* and *Moses und Aron* to name but a few).[189] In Burger's case, this work is a rare, direct reference to Judaism and his Jewish identity and thus, serves as an important artifact for future research.

3.3 Sketches and others (Catalogue 1.2.6 – 1.2.7.)

3.3.1. Works for stage (1.2.6.)

The vast majority of Julius Burger's career was directly associated with theatres of the operatic and lighter operetta tradition in a multitude of roles. This diverse portfolio spanned from prominent European theatres and included a twenty-year tenure at the Metropolitan Opera where he served as assistant conductor, repetiteur and coach, composer, arranger and even a short period as a musician in the company's orchestra. This provided him with an intimate knowledge of the theatre and his musical works in this area were a logical progression for the composer. There are three known works in this category which all derive from Burger's tenure with the Metropolitan Opera in the mid-1950s. These include the music score for the one act ballet *Vittorio* (1954), the revised orchestration for the company's English adaptation of Offenbach's *La Périchole* (1956) and four entr'actes which were incorporated into the 1957 Peter Brook production of Tchaikovsky's *Eugene Onegin*.

---

188 Ernest Bloch, Sacred Service (Avodat Hakodesh), Volume 7: Masterworks of Prayer, Milken Archive of Jewish Music, https://www.milkenarchive.org/music/volumes/view/masterworks-of-prayer/work/sacred-service-avodat-hakodesh/, Accessed 14 January 2022.

189 Kenneth H. Marcus, 'Chapter 5- Judaism revisited: Schoenberg's Jewish works from Part II – The private and public spheres, 1936–1951', *Schoenberg and Hollywood Modernism*, Cambridge University Press, 2016, p.161-184.

These works draw on Burger's aptitude in arranging, which were mastered through his Radio Potpourri commissions for the Berlin Funkstunde and the BBC as well as his work with CBS under Andre Kostelanetz and Arthur Fiedler. These qualities are embedded in the score for the 1954 one act ballet in three scenes titled *Vittorio* (Box 22, No. 1.2.6.1.).

The story is rooted in the classic operatic tradition and is set in Renaissance Italy. A princess arrives from the Isle of Spain in Italy in order to enter into an arranged marriage of alliance to the aged Duke of Montefiore. Instead, she falls in love with his handsome grandson (Vittorio) who is already betrothed to the character of Fiamma. The volatile Spanish princess becomes enraged and attempts to abduct Vittorio which prompts his protector, the sorceress and fortune teller La Magilana to hide the young prince in neighbouring castle's crypt. After a failed attempt to locate Vittorio, the Spanish princess returns to wait at the Palace of Montefiore where preparations have been made for her marriage to the aged Duke. After Vittorio and Fiamma re-emerge at the palace, a climatic dual ensues between the princess and La Magilana in which both are killed. The work ends with a love scene between Vittorio and Fiamma after which the prince is crowned as the new ruler of the dukedom and as majestic party closes the third scene.[190]

The work was initiated from the Metropolitan's general manager, Rudolf Bing, who wanted to revitalise the company's neglected ballet division and marks the Metropolitan's first new ballet commission since the 1926 work *Skyscrapers* (choreographed by Sammy Lee, music by Robert Edmond Jones).[191] The task was given to company choreographer and dancer Zachary Solov to conceive the storyline and choreograph the new commission to a score arranged and orchestrated by Burger. The score is a pastiche which utilises thematic material from no less than twelve operatic works by Giuseppe Verdi. The score includes music from *Aroldo* (1857), *La Battaglio die Legnano* (1849), *I Lombardi* (1843), *Alzira* (1845), *Un Giorno di Regno* [*Il Finto Stanislao*] (1840), *Giovanna d'Arco* (1845), *Luisa Miller* (1849) as well as material from ballet music within the operas of *Macbeth* (1865 version), *Il Trovatore* (1853), *Vespri Siciliani* (1855), *Ernani* (1844) and *Don Carlo* (1867).[192] These were then arranged into a cohesive work, supplemented with original material from Burger.

Vittorio was premiered on 15 December 1954, followed by a production of Richard Strauss's *Salome* (1905), and was performed six times between December 1954 and January of the following year. Notably, the pairing marked the Metropolitan debuts of numerous performers including conductor

---

190 Thomas R. Dash, "'Vittorio' and 'Salome': Metropolitan Opera," *Women's Wear Daily*, 16 December 1954.

191 John Martin, "The Dance: Premiere – The Metropolitan Opera Presents a Ballet," *New York Times*, 12 December 1954, Vol. CIV, No.35,386, Section. X, p.18.

192 Julius Burger, *Vittorio* (1954), Ballet in 3 scenes by Zachary Solov, music by Julius Burger, EaZ-001-03-00548, Box 22, No. 1.2.6.1.1., Stage Works, 1.2.6., Julius Burger (Bürger) Collection, Exilarte Zentrum Archiv der mdw, Vienna, Austria.

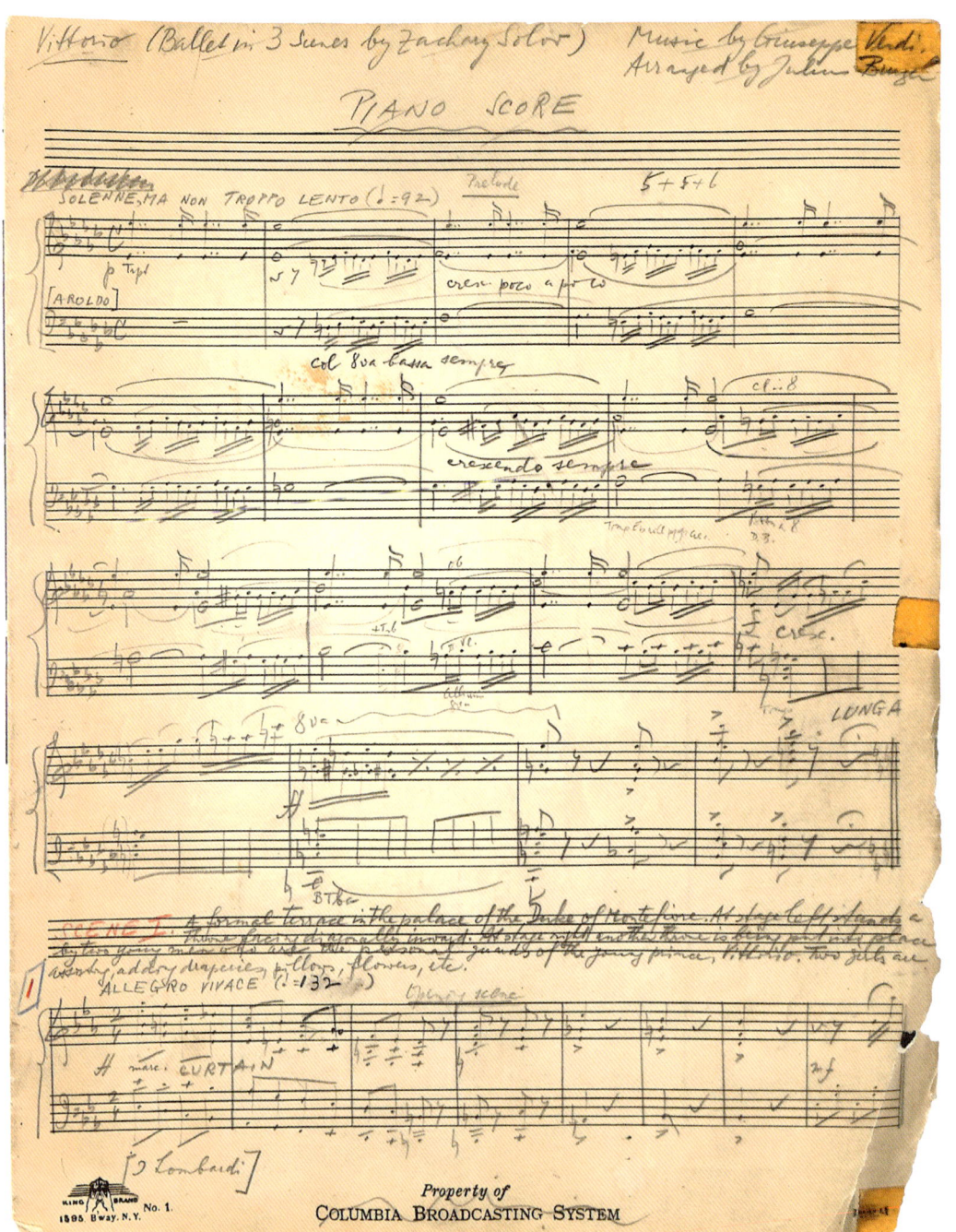

Manuscript score of the 1954 three-act ballet *Vittorio* – created in collaboration with Metropolitan ballet master Zachary Solov. © A-Weaz

Playbill for the second performance of *Vittorio* (22 December 1954). The production marked conductor Dimitri Mitropoulos' debut with the MET and his engagement conducting a ballet.
© Private collection of Dr. R. H. Ross

Dimitri Mitropoulos (1896–1960).[193] Reviews of the work were largely positive with praise for the musical arrangement: *"The orchestral arrangement was coordinated by J. Burger, who performed a brilliant task in weaving the shreds of patchwork into a beautiful mosaic of music. ... The score sounds unified and fits the theme and mood of the story as if Verdi had composed it especially for last night's Tour de force."*[194] A second review in the *New York Times* described the work as *"mov[ing] with the speed and energy of a Hollywood thriller, and there is scarcely a breather for anybody from curtain to curtain."*[195]

An incomplete manuscript piano score of this work is preserved with notes in Exilarte in Vienna while a complete, formalised version of the piano score with staging notes is preserved among the Zachary Solov Papers in the New York Public Library's Archives.[196]

Two years after the success of *Vittorio*, Burger was engaged once again as orchestrator and arranger for the company's revised English language version of Offenbach's 1874 revised, three act opéra bouffe *La Périchole*. This new adaptation utilised a translated libretto from the original French by Meilhac and Halévy's to English by playwright Maurice Valency (1903–1996). It also included fach changes to several prominent characters including a coloratura soprano instead of mezzo-soprano for the title role (played by Patrice Munsel), a high baritone in the place of a tenor for the role of Piquillo (played by Theodor Uppman) and included new music written for a comic tenor for the formerly spoken role of the Old Prisoner.

The new version was prepared by conductors Jean Morel (1903–1975), who also conducted the premiere, and fellow Schreker student Ignace Strasfogel (1909–1994). It was staged by Cyril Ritchard (1898–1977), who also performed the role of Don Andres de Ribeira. The score was arranged and orchestrated by Burger and included interpolations from other works. His aptitude at arranging and orchestrating stems from his experiences with the Berlin Funkstunde, the BBC in London and more recent work with CBS. A specific example is the 1934 work *Life of Offenbach* in which Burger conveys the composer's life through a series of biographic vignettes while drawing on music from his more popular operettas including *La Périchole*.

The Metropolitan premiered their version on 21 December 1956. It was a success with audiences and critics alike through the 1956–57 season. It enjoyed twenty-one performances as well as a further nine performances the following season in-

---

193 *Vittorio* was premiered 15 December 1954 at the Metropolitan Opera, New York City. It was paired with a production of Richard Strauss' *Salome* starring Christel Goltz in her Met debut. The premiere also marked the Met debut of conductor Dimitri Mitropoulos. Source: Playbill for *Vittorio* at the Metropolitan Opera, New York, Playbill, 22 December 1954, p.10-11.

194 Thomas R. Dash, " 'Vittorio' and Salome' – Metropolitan Opera," *Women's Wear Daily*, 16 December 1954, from the Julius Burger (Bürger) Collection, Exilarte Zentrum Archiv der mdw, Vienna, Austria.

195 John Martin, "Solov's 'Vittorio' is Danced at the MET – New, Lavish Ballet Offered in 'Grand Manner' by Troupe of Excellent Performers," *New York Times*, 16 December 1954, Vo. CIV, No.35,390, Amusements section, p.49.

196 Julius Burger, *Vittorio*, b.13 f.2-3, Series IV: Scores and Music, from Zachary Solov Papers, Jerome Robbins Dance Division, New York Public Library, Call No. (S) *MGZMD 261.

cluding a NBC live telecast on 28 January 1958.[197] The work stayed in the company's repertoire until the early 1970s.

Other works for stage productions include four original entr'actes for the Metropolitan's 1957 Peter Brook production of Tchaikovsky's three-act opera *Eugene Onegin*.[198] These included musical themes which were suggested by conductor Dimitri Mitropoulos which Burger then adapted into his orchestrations. They were utilised in twenty-one performances between 28 October 1957 and 3 April 1959 until the production was revived in 1964 and subsequently removed under conductor Thomas Schippers.[199] The reception of the entr'actes was more mixed than Burger's previous works for the company with one critic noting *"[t]he interludes quote Tchaikovsky so extensively and are so hopped up in instrumentation that they sound like reprises plugging the show's hit tunes."*[200]

Two sources have indicated there may have been attempts by Burger in composing his own operas. The first stems from his studies under Engelbert Humperdinck in Berlin – utilising Goethe's Faust as a thematic basis.[201] A second source, stemming from an interview with a close family associate, indicated Burger may have composed scenes utilising text from friend Ödön von Horváth's *Geschichten aus dem Wiener Wald* before the latter's untimely death in 1938.[202] Further investigation is required to substantiate these leads.

3.4 Radio Music (Catalogue 1.3; BBC Box 1 – 6)

While all of Julius Burger's compositions deserve more recognition, his large-scale radio creations for the Berlin Funkstunde, and particularly the BBC, deserve special consideration. These works, which Burger deemed 'Radio Potpourri', hold the peculiar position of being broadcast to the largest audiences to date while equally being the least researched

---

197 The Met's production of La Périchole was telecast by NBC studios from their Manhattan studio on 26 January 1958 in a matinee performance as part of the Omnibus series. Source: "La Périchole," Performance 29, 26 January 1958, Metopera database, Metropolitan Opera Archives, CID: 176920, keyword search 'La Périchole', URL: http://69.18.170.204/archives/frame.htm, accessed 13 April 2021.

198 The English translated version was directed by Peter Brook, designed by Rolf Gerard, and choreographed by Zachary Solov. The production starred George London in the title role as well as Lucine Amara as Tatiana and Richard Tucker as Lensky. "Eugene Onegin," Performance 9, 28 October 1957, Metopera database, Metropolitan Opera Archives, CID: 176000, keyword search 'Eugene Onegin', URL: http://69.18.170.204/archives/frame.htm, accessed 14 April 2021.

199 "Eugene Onegin," Performance 31, 15 February 1964, Metopera database, Metropolitan Opera Archives, CID: 197250, keyword search 'Eugene Onegin', URL: http://archives.metoperafamily.org/archives/frame.htm, accessed 14 April 2021.

200 Howard Taubman, "Opera: 'Eugene Onegin'" *New York Times*, 29 October 1957, p.36.

201 Albrecht Dümling, "Joseph Schmidt sang seine Lieder: Der Schreker-Schüler Julius Bürger," Program notes for Rundfunk-Sinfonieorchester Berlin, *Konzert mit Werken von Julius Bürger*, cond. Simone Young, cello Maya Beiser, baritone Michael Kraus, 29 September 1994, Jesus-Christus-Kirche Berlin.

202 Dr. Trude Zörer, "Interview by Ryan Hugh Ross on the life of Julius Burger (Bürger)," opening conversation, 30 October 2019.

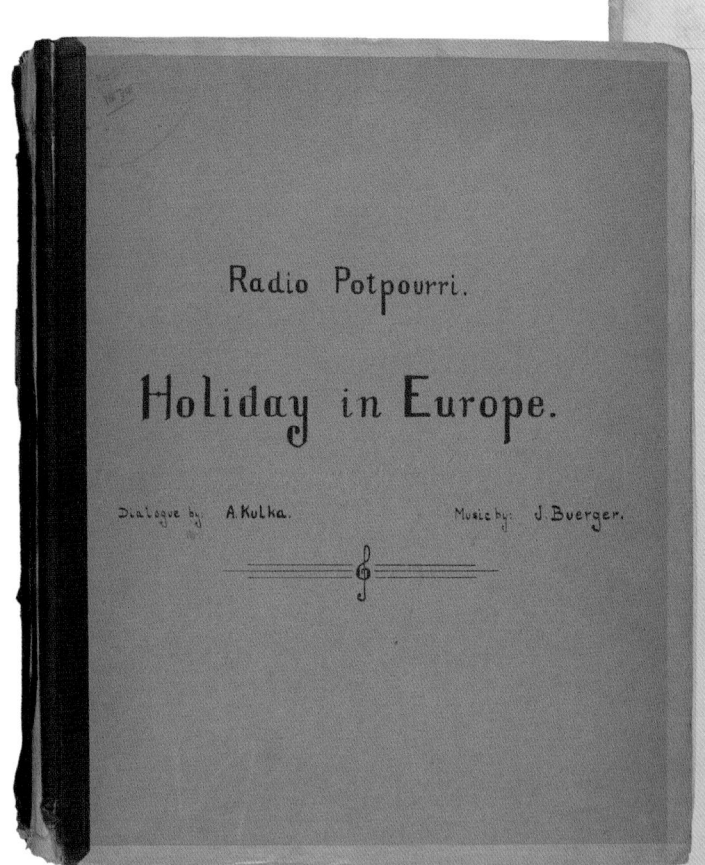

Cover and dedication page for the 1934 Radio Potpourri *Holiday in Europe*. The work was created by Burger in collaboration with writing partner Artur Kulka and is dedicated to BBC Variety department director Eric Maschwitz. © A-Weaz

of his œuvre. One key reason for this oversight is due to the held assumption the majority of the works, which were largely produced before the Second World War, were among the scores of BBC's Broadcasting House destroyed when a German bomb detonated in the building's music library on 15 October 1940.[203] However, a large collection of the manuscript scores were recently rediscovered in early 2019 among the vast archival collections at the BBC's Perivale Sheet Music Library in London.

The concept of musical potpourri is not new (as composers had been making potpourris since the mid-eighteenth century) and appears in many similar forms such as divertissements, rhapsodies, and fantasias. It shares many characteristics with pasticcio operas as well as musical accompaniment practices in silent film cinemas of the early twentieth century. However, Burger's development of the genre took what were usually ten-minute melanges of music and expanded them for radio to into hour-long epics around a central theme with narration. Radio Potpourri are generally self-contained works which utilise themes or sections from existing musical works which are then combined with incidental music around a central theme. Scripted narration commonly accompanied the piece to supplement the performance. They are generally scored for orchestra with vocal soloists and chorus as well as instrumental soli as required.

The earliest known example of a composition in this genre by Burger, titled *Hallo London, Here's Berlin* (1932) stems from his tenure at the Berlin Funkstunde.[204] The work, now lost, featured light orchestral and vocal music from popular German musical comedies and operettas of the period. It was broadcast simultaneously in Germany and the UK from the company's Berlin studios through a partnership with the BBC.[205]

The Radio Potpourri was developed in a period where many artists were working on the question posed by the technological advances of radio, specifically how to retool traditional art forms for presentation via mass media. Some examples from Germany's late Weimar period include Paul Hindemith's "Gebrauchsmusik" works for radio (*Der Lindberghflug*, a cantata composed with Kurt Weill on text by Bertolt Brecht),[206] Austrian Karl Kraus' reimagined presentations of Offenbach operettas as well as the experiments with radio plays (Hörspiel) by novelists like Alfred Döbin (*The Story of Franz Bieberkopf*, a derived from his successful novel *Berlin Alexanderplatz*).[207] Likewise, there was also some early ex-

---

203 David Hendy, "The Bombing of Broadcasting House," BBC online, URL: https://www.bbc.com/historyofthebbc/100-voices/ww2/bh-bombs/, Accessed 12 January 2022.

204 Julius Burger, "Letter to Eric Maschwitz," 21 January 1935, From Burger, Julius. 31-42. R27/40/2. BBC Music-General: Burger, Julius. BBC Written Archives Centre, Reading, England.

205 Contributor, "Hallo London, Here's Berlin," *Radio Times*, 11 November 1932, Issue 476, p.44r.

206 Britannica, The Editors of Encyclopaedia. "Paul Hindemith". *Encyclopaedia Britannica*, 24 Dec. 2021, https://www.britannica.com/biography/Paul-Hindemith. Accessed 17 February 2022.

207 Peter Jelavich, *Berlin Alexanderplatz: Radio, Film, and the Death of Weimar Culture*, (Berkeley: University of California Press, 2006), p.62-125.

perimentation at fledgling BBC in the form of radio operas by Ezra Pound, *The Testament of François Villon* (1931)[208] and *Cavalcanti* (1932).[209]

While Burger's radio works vary in length and thematic nature, they can be delineated into three main columns: Grand potpourri (categorised as such for its greatly expanded use of musical content and performance length of approximately one hour), Miniature potpourri (these most commonly resemble the original potpourri archetype, are approximately ten minutes in duration and can be performed separately as a single piece or multiple 'mini' potpourri can be grouped together to form chapters of a larger, segmented construction for broadcast) and the Chapter potpourri (a larger, serial potpourri programme made up of smaller segments or chapters comprised of Miniature potpourri).

Of the surviving works rediscovered at the BBC's Perivale Sheet Music Library, the most numerous are the Grand potpourri. These deserve particular focus for their inventive use of narration, sound effects, and intricate incorporation of existing musical themes woven together to form a comprehensive work. They fall into four further categories which are grouped together on similar thematic subjects. Geographic potpourris utilise music from a travel itinerary overlaid with intermittent dialogue and sound effects to delineate the journey. There are several surviving examples. The earliest is the 1934 work *Holiday in Europe* (BBC Box 1, No. 1.3.2.)[210] which followed a honeymooning couple as they travel throughout continental Europe. *The Empire Sings!* (1938; BBC Box 3, No. 1.3.7.)[211] is a musical tour of the British Empire's colonial territories and dominions as they were in 1938 while *New World Rhapsody*

---

208 *Testament of François Villon* was broadcast by the BBC on the National Programme 26 October 1931 at 9:50PM and again the following day on BBC London regional programme at 8:45PM. Source: Contributor, *Testament of François Villon*, Radio Times, 23 October 1931, Vol.33, Issue 421, p.276, 287.

209 *Cavalcanti* was not broadcast in Pound's lifetime. Source: Margaret Fisher, *Ezra Pound's Radio operas: The BBC Experiments, 1931–1933* (Cambridge: Massachusetts Institute of Technology, 2002).

210 *Holiday in Europe* was completed 2 April 1934 in Vienna and includes dialogue by blacklisted Jewish author, Arthur Kulka. Known broadcasts on the BBC include: 17 & 18 July 1934 and 9 January 1938. (Source: *Radio Times*, Issue No. 563, p. 105, 112 & No. 745, p.18.) A conductor score as well as a reduced piano/vocal score, both in manuscript, can be found in the Burger collection at the Exilarte Zentrum Archiv der mdw: Julius Burger, *Holiday in Europe* (1934), autograph manuscripts, BBC No: MSS1878-Buerger, EaZ-035-03-00020, BBC Box 1, No. 1.2.3., Julius Burger (Bürger) Collection, Exilarte Zentrum Archiv der mdw, Vienna, Austria.

211 *The Empire Sings!* (also known as *Songs of the British Empire*) was Completed 5 April 1938 at Juan les Pins, France after the abandoned trip to vote against Austria's plebiscite vote of annexation (Anschluss). Known broadcasts on the BBC include: 22 & 23 May 1938 and 18 February 1940. (Sources: *Radio Times*, Issue No. 764, p. 8, 28, 30; Issue No. 855, p.15. A manuscript conductor score can be found in the Burger collection at the Exilarte Zentrum Archiv der mdw: Julius Burger, *The Empire Sings!* (1938), autograph manuscript, BBC No.: MSS6401. Buerger, EaZ-035-03-00021, BBC Box 3, No. 1.3.7., Julius Burger (Bürger) Collection, Exilarte Zentrum Archiv der mdw, Vienna, Austria.

Cover to the manuscript score of Life of [Jacques] Offenbach (1934). This particular score was only recently unearthed during a final survey of BBC archival collection in preparation for the Radio Potpourri œuvre's relocation to the Exilarte Archiv der mdw in late 2022. Right: Manuscript score examples from Burger's 'Ode to Offenbach'. © A-Weaz

(1942; BBC Box 3, No. 1.3.8.)[212] is an exploration of the music and cultures of North and South America.

Two examples survive of the Biographic potpourri category including *Life of Offenbach* (1934; BBC Box 1, No. 1.3.1.)[213] and *Johann Strauss: A Biography in Music* (1936; BBC Box 5, No. 1.3.16. – 17.).[214] These utilise music by a chosen composer coupled with narration to convey the story of their life through a series of musical vignettes. They appear to have had lasting influence on BBC programming throughout the 1930s and 1940s, prompting other musical staff to follow with their own versions in the style. Several examples include *Puccini: the Man and his Music,*[215] and *Mendelssohn in En-*

---

212 *New World Rhapsody* was completed in early 1942 while Burger was living in New York City. Known broadcasts on the BBC include: 3 & 5 March 1944 and 20 August 1944. (Sources: *Radio Times*, 12 February 1944, Vol.82, Issue 1065, p.6, 16; *Radio Times*, 18 August 1944, Vol.84, Issue 1090, p.6.).

A manuscript conductor score in three books can be found in the Burger collection at the Exilarte Zentrum Archiv der mdw: Julius Burger, *New World Rhapsody* (1942), manuscript conductor's score in three parts, BBC No.: TO 1370 Buerger, EaZ-035-03-00015 – 00016; 00001, BBC Box 3, No. 1.3.8., Julius Burger (Bürger) Collection, Exilarte Zentrum Archiv der mdw, Vienna, Austria.

213 *The Life of Offenbach* was completed in partnership with writer Arthur Kulka in 1934 in Vienna, Austria. It was first broadcast on 7 January 1935 on BBC National Service at 9PM with a second performance the following evening at 8PM also on the BBC National Service. Four subsequent known broadcasts include 27 February 1938 on BBC National Service at 9:25PM, 3 September 1944 on BBC Home Service at 9:30PM, 5 November 1944 at 10PM and 16 April 1950 at 4PM- both on the BBC Home Service. (*Radio Times*: 4 January 1934. Vol.46, Issue 588. p.7, 28, 31, 34; 25 February 1938, Vol.58, Issue 752, p.20; 1 September 1944, Vol.84, Issue 1092, p.6; 3 November 1944, Vol. 85, Issue 1101, p.6; 14 April 1950, Vol. 107, Issue 1383, p.14;)

Manuscripts can be found in the Burger collection at the Exilarte Zentrum Archiv der mdw: Julius Burger, *Life of Offenbach* (1934), hand copied manuscript orchestral parts, BBC No.: MSS2891, Buerger, EaZ-035-03-00002, BBC Box 1, No. 1.3.1., Julius Burger (Bürger) Collection, Exilarte Zentrum Archiv der mdw, Vienna, Austria.

214 *Johann Strauss: A Biography in Music* was first broadcast on 15 November 1936 on BBC Regional Service at 5:30PM with a second performance on 17 November 1936 at 8PM on BBC National Service. It was broadcast a further 6 times: 12 March 1939 on Daventry Regional Service at 6.50PM, 13 March 1939 on BBC Regional Service at 9PM, 19 July 1942 on BBC Home Service at 9:30PM, 14 May 1944 on BBC Home Service at 10:50PM, 6 August 1944 on BBC Home Service at 9:35PM and 6 November 1949on BBC Home Service at 6:45PM. (*Radio Times*: 13 November 1936, Issue 685. p.28, 44; 10 March 1939, Vol.62, Issue 806, p.20, 30, 33; 17 July 1942, Vol. 76, p.6; 12 May 1944, Vol. 83, Issue 1076, p.6; 4 August 1944, Vol. 84, Issue 1088, p.6; 4 November 1949, Vol.105, Issue 1360, p.18.)

Manuscript parts can be found in the Burger collection at the Exilarte Zentrum Archiv der mdw: Julius Burger, *Johann Strauss: A Biography in Music* (aka *Homage to Johann Strauss: A Strauss Potpourri*) (1936), manuscript score in 2 parts, BBC No.: MSS3771, Buerger, EaZ-035-03-00011 – 00012, BBC Box 5, No. 1.3.16. – 1.3.17., Julius Burger (Bürger) Collection, Exilarte Zentrum Archiv der mdw, Vienna, Austria.

215 The first performance was on the BBC National Programme 29 March 1936 at 9PM and was arranged by Mark Lubbock. (*Puccini: The Man and his Music, Radio Times*, No. 652, 27 March 1936, p.20) It was later revived for broadcast several times throughout the decade including on 7 & 9 November 1937 (*Puccini: The Man and his Music, Radio Times*, 5 November 1937, Vol.57, Issue 736, p.38, 46.) and 20 March 1940 (*Puccini: The Man and his Music, Radio Times*, 15 March 1940, Vol. 66, Issue 859, p.26.)

gland: A Musical Biography[216] among others. Equally, a series of five- and six-part biographic presentations were also produced following the two Biographic potpourris on numerous other composers.

The Historic potpourri present music associated with an historic event (such as a coronation, military conflict) or the historic progression of a particular location for its thematic subject. Two surviving examples from this category include the miniature potpourri *Boer War Songs* (1937; BBC Box 5, No. 1.3.19.),[217] which utilises popular wartime ballads as its musical sources, *Regimental Marches* (1938; BBC Box 5, No. 1.3.21.)[218] and the grand potpourri *Themes of London* (1937; BBC Box 6, No. 1.3.24.).[219] The latter is a musical representation of London throughout the ages. It opens with an introduction utilising the Westminster chimes before transporting the listener to a market square in the Elizabethan era. The work then progresses to Baroque London (incorporations of Henry Purcell, Georg Friedrich Händel, and folk melodies from the British Isles), a Victorian ball (ballroom dance music and polkas) to Hyde Park and the music halls of the Edwardian period (incorporations of military marches as well as popular music hall ballads) until reaching an exciting climax

---

216 Broadcast 28 August 1938 at 9:05PM on National Programme and described as "A musical biography, with special reference to the composer's visits to the British Isles, written and spoken by Wilfred Rooke Ley, Music selected by Mark H. Lubbock and Max Robertson." It goes on to describe the piece itself: "Mendelssohn came to England in 1829, on the first of many visits. Several works which will be heard in this programme are examples of his close connection with this country. They include the Scherzo in G minor from his Octet for strings, Op. 20, orchestrated by the composer and incorporated in his First Symphony which he conducted on his first appearance in England; the famous 'Spring Song', composed while on a visit to friends who resided at Denmark Hill; his 'Scottish' Symphony and 'Hebrides' Overture, which show how deeply the scenery of Britain had influenced him; and Elijah, commissioned for and performed at the Birmingham Musical Festival in 1846." Source: Contributor. 'Mendelssohn in England', *Radio Times*, 26 August 1938, Vol.60, Issue 778, p.22.

217 *Boer War Songs* was first broadcast on 14 March 1937 on BBC Regional Service at 7:10PM as the 12th installment of the programme *Victorian Melodies*. (Contributor, "Boer War Songs," *Radio Times*, 12 March 1937, Vol. 54, Issue 702, p.22.)

A manuscript conductor score can be found in the Burger collection at the Exilarte Zentrum Archiv der mdw: Julius Burger, *Selection of Boer War Songs* (1937), autograph manuscript conductor's score, BBC No.: MMS4242, Buerger, EaZ-035-03-00018, BBC Box 5, No. 1.3.19., Julius Burger (Bürger) Collection, Exilarte Zentrum Archiv der mdw, Vienna, Austria.

218 *Regimental Marches* (aka *Selection of Military* Marches) was first broadcast 18 September 1938 on BBC National Service at 9:05PM as the 4th installment of the Chapter potpourri *Songs of the British Isles*. (Contributor, "Regimental Marches," *Radio Times*, 16 September 1938, Vol. 60, Issue 781, p.22)

A manuscript conductor score can be found in the Burger collection at the Exilarte Zentrum Archiv der mdw: Julius Burger, *Selection of Military Marches* (1938), autograph manuscript conductor's score, BBC No. MSS6782, Buerger, EaZ-035-03-00022, BBC Box 5, No. 1.3.21., Julius Burger (Bürger) Collection, Exilarte Zentrum Archiv der mdw, Vienna, Austria.

219 *Themes of London* (aka *London: A Radio Potpourri*) was first broadcast 8 December 1937 at 7:15PM on BBC National Service with a second performance on 10 December 1937 at 9PM on BBC Regional Service. (Contributor, "Themes of London," *Radio Times*, 3 December 1937, Vol.57, Issue 740, p.12, 54, 80).

A manuscript conductor score in 2 books with production notes can be found in the Burger collection at the Exilarte Zentrum Archiv der mdw: Julius Burger, *London: A Radio Potpourri* (1937), autograph manuscript conductor's score in two books, BBC No.: MSS5770, Buerger, EaZ-035-03-00025 – 00026, BBC Box 6, No. 1.3.24., Julius Burger (Bürger) Collection, Exilarte Zentrum Archiv der mdw, Vienna, Austria.

Advert for Julius Burger's *Holiday in Europe* (1934).
© Radio Times, 13 July 1934, Vol. 44, Issue 563, p.112.

Advert for Julius Burger's *Life of Offenbach* (1934).
© Radio Times, 4 January 1935, Vol. 46, Issue 588, p.34.

Promotional photo for the 1935 premiere of *City of Music* featuring a youthful Julius Burger.
© Radio Times, 19 July 1935, Vol. 48, Issue 616, p.50.

Advert for Julius Burger's *City of Music* (1935)
© Radio Times, 19 July 1935, Vol. 48, Issue 616, p.40.

Advert for Julius Burger's *World Tour* (1935)
© Radio Times, 22 November 1935, Vol. 49, Issue 634, p.64.

Advert for Julius Burger's *Liebestraum* (1935)
© Radio Times, 31 January 1936, Vol. 50, Issue 644, p.36.

Advert for Julius Burger's *Festival of Folk Music* (1936)
© Radio Times, 1 May 1936, Vol. 51, Issue 657, p.26.

Advert for Julius Burger's *Johann Strauss (1825–1899): A Biography in Music* (1936)
© Radio Times, 13 Nov. 1936, Vol. 52, Issue 685, p.42.

Advert for Julius Burger's *Themes of London* (1937)
© Radio Times, 3 December 1937, Vol. 57, Issue 740, p.54.

Advert for Julius Burger's *World Tour* (1937)
© Radio Times, 7 February 1937, Vo. 54, Issue 697, p.21.

Advert for Julius Burger's *City of Music* (1935)
© Radio Times, 28 January 1938, Vol. 58, Issue 748, p.20.

Radio Times cover for the 1945 Victory in Europe week.
Radio Times, 10 May 1945, Vol. 87, Issue 1138 - Cover.

Advert for Julius Burger's *Victory Rhapsody* aka *The Nations Sing!* (1945). The work premiered the evening of 13 May 1945 (9:30PM) on the BBC Home Service – only five days after the unconditional surrender of the Nazi regime. [It was reprised on 17 May 1945 (2PM) on the General Forces Service and was broadcast three more times between late May and November of that year.]
© Radio Times, 16 Nov. 1945, Vol. 89, Issue 1155, p.10.

in contemporary 1930s London. For the final sequence, Burger utilised two jazz-influenced ballads, which would have possibly been heard in clubs and bars of London's Mayfair and Piccadilly Circus, "On your Toes" and "I'm in a Dancing Mood." Another noteworthy inclusion in this category is the 1945 Radio Potpourri *The Nations Sing (or Victory Rhapsody)*.[220] The work, now lost, was part of BBC's VE celebration programming in the days following the Allied victory in 1945. *The Nations Sing!* incorporates music from across the British Empire and includes a final 'parade' montage utilising thematic material from the national anthems of Allied nations.

The fourth 'General' category contains works which do not share common characteristics with other potpourri works. One such example is the 1936 work *Festival of Folk Music* (BBC Box 3, No. 1.3.7.).[221] The premise is based on a pan-European competition held in the Royal Albert Hall in which each country presents a troupe performing selections of traditional folk dance and music from their nation. This is then supplemented with witty, impromptu-style narration by a radio commentator. The premise is reminiscent of the modern-day Eurovision Song Contest.

A large number of Miniature potpourri were also composed during this period along with dozens of arrangements and orchestrations for other programmed productions. Many of Burger's surviving Miniature potpourri are incorporations of music centred around the composer who originally produced them. Some surviving examples include *A Potpourri of Melodies of Leo Fall* (1934; NNC Box 1, No. 1.3.3.),[222] *A Pot-*

---

220 *The Nations Sing!* was first broadcast on 13 May 1945 on the BBC Home Service at 9:30PM shortly followed by a performance on 17 May 1945 at 2PM on the General Forces Service. Three further known broadcasts include 20 May 1945 at 9:30PM & 18 November 1945 at 9:30PM (both on the BBC Home Service) and 20 November 1945 at 1:15PM on the BBC Light Programme. (Contributor, "The Nations Sing," *Radio Times*: Vol.87, Issue 1128.p.12, 21; Vol. 87, Issue 1129, p.10; Vol.89, Issue 1155, p.10, 15.) The location of this work is unknown.

221 *Festival of Folk Music* was described in its May 1936 listing in *Radio Times*: "Music knows no national frontiers, yet folk music almost invariably is as characteristic as a flag. Fascinating music it is, too, full of melody and rhythm, and expressive of the soil and the joys and pains of love. This evening' Dr. Buerger has collected the folk music of eleven countries: England, Italy, Germany, Czechoslovakia, France, Poland, Norway, Spain, Austria, Russia, and Hungary, and he has welded this medley of tunes into an hour's potpourri. An interesting feature of this broadcast is that the songs will be sung in the language of their origin." Source: Contributor, "Festival of Folk Music," *Radio Times*, 1 May 1936, Vol. 57, Issue 657, p.24.

A manuscript conductors score in 3 books can be found in the Julius Burger Collection at the Exilarte Zentrum Archiv der mdw: Julius Burger, *Festival of Folk Music* (1936), autograph manuscript conductor's score in 3 books, BBC No.: MSS2903:A-F, Buerger, EaZ-035-03-00027 – 00029, BBC Box 2, No. 1.3.6., Julius Burger (Bürger) Collection, Exilarte Zentrum Archiv der mdw, Vienna, Austria.

222 *A Potpourri of Melodies by Leo Fall* was composed from the 7th to 24th of February 1934 in Vienna. It was first broadcast on 4 November 1934 on the BBC London Regional Programme at 6:30PM. Source: Contributor, "A Potpourri of Leo Fall's Melodies," *Radio Times*, 2 November 1934, Vol.45, Issue 579, p.24.) A manuscript conductor score can be found in the Burger collection at the Exilarte Zentrum Archiv der mdw: Julius Burger, *A Potpourri of Melodies by Leo Fall* (1934), autograph manuscript conductor's score, BBC No.: MSS6497, Bürger, EaZ-035-03-00003, BBC Box 1, No. 1.3.3., Julius Burger (Bürger) Collection, Exilarte Zentrum Archiv der mdw, Vienna, Austria.

pourri of Melodies of Edmund Eysler (1936; BBC Box 4, No. 1.3.14.),²²³ *A Potpourri of Schubert Waltzes* (1936; BBC Box 2, No 1.3.5.),²²⁴ *A Potpourri of Melodies by Edmond Audran* (1936; BBC Box 2, No. 1.3.4.),²²⁵ and *A Potpourri of Archibald Joyce's Waltzes* (possibly 1936; BBC Box 4, No. 1.3.11.).²²⁶

The Radio Potpourri genre was a success in its use by the BBC Variety Department which had only been created in mid-1933 with Erich Maschwitz as its first director. These commissions are significant for several reasons. They serve as a cross-cultural device which was previously not used in the United Kingdom. After further development in the Corporation, these works also influenced later programming until the department was disbanded in 1967.²²⁷ The timeframe in which the works were commissioned provide important insight into the composer's exile while equally serving as a lifeline. He was unable to gain permission to reside in the UK except for short periods in London and wrote much of the potpourri from short-let stays and hotels throughout Vienna, Brussels, Paris, and greater France.

Finally, while the BBC had a large number of prominent émigré artists in their employ in the 1930s (for example, Walter Goehr, Leo Wurmser, Ernst Hermann Meyer, Artur Willner, Franz Reizenstein, Berthold Goldschmidt and Mátyás Seiber),²²⁸ they generally did not have their works performed or commissioned by the Corporation and occupied various positions in the corporation including administrative and editorial positions. According to Musicologist Florian Sheding,

---

223 *A Potpourri of Melodies of Edmund Eysler* was likely composed from Vienna early in Burger's association with the BBC. It is undated. No broadcast dates have been yet located. A manuscript conductor score can be found in the Burger collection at the Exilarte Zentrum Archiv der mdw: Julius Burger, *A Potpourri of Melodies of Edmund Eysler* (Undated), autograph manuscript conductor's score, BBC No.: MSS2135-Bürger, EaZ-035-03-00009, BBC Box 4, No. 1.3.14., Julius Burger (Bürger) Collection, Exilarte Zentrum Archiv der mdw, Vienna, Austria.

224 *A Potpourri of Schubert Waltzes* has been dated to 1936 through archival documentation from the BBC Written Archive in Caversham, England. A manuscript conductor score and a piano reduction score can be found in the Burger collection at the Exilarte Zentrum Archiv der mdw: Julius Burger, *A Potpourri of Schubert Waltzes* (1936), autograph manuscript conductor's score, BBC No.: MSS 3149, Buerger, EaZ-035-03-00014, BBC Box 2, No. 1.3.5., Julius Burger (Bürger) Collection, Exilarte Zentrum Archiv der mdw, Vienna, Austria.

225 *A Potpourri of Melodies by Edmond Audran* was composed from Alt Aussee, Austria in 1936 as indicated in the manuscript score. Definitive broadcasting dates have not been confirmed. Two full manuscript scores and inst. parts can be found in the Burger collection at the Exilarte Zentrum Archiv der mdw: Julius Burger, *A Potpourri of Melodies by Edmond Audran* (1936 in Alt Aussee, Austria), BBC No.: MSS3496, Buerger, EaZ-035-03-00013, BBC Box 2, No. 1.3.4., Julius Burger (Bürger) Collection, Exilarte Zentrum Archiv der mdw, Vienna, Austria.

226 *Potpourri of Archibald Joyce's Waltzes* possibly dates from 1936 but is yet to be confirmed. Definitive broadcasting dates have not been confirmed. A manuscript conductor score, individual instrumental parts and chorus parts can be found in the Burger collection at the Exilarte Zentrum Archiv der mdw: Julius Burger, *Archibald Joyce Waltz Potpourri* (1935?), BBC No.: MSS 2340, Buerger, EaZ-035-03-00006, BBC Box 4, No. 1.3.11., Julius Burger (Bürger) Collection, Exilarte Zentrum Archiv der mdw, Vienna, Austria.

227 Martin Dibbs, "1956–67: Sound into Vision; Popular into Pop," from *Radio Fun and the BBC Variety Department, 1922–67: Comedy and Popular Music on Air*, Palgrave Studies in the History of the Media, (Cham: Palgrave Macmillan, 2019), p.229-274.

228 Florian Scheding, 'Problematic Tendencies': Émigré Composers in London, 1933–1945", *The Impact of Nazism on Twentieth-Century Music*. Levi, E. (ed.). (Vienna: Böhlau Verlag, 2014), p. 247-271.

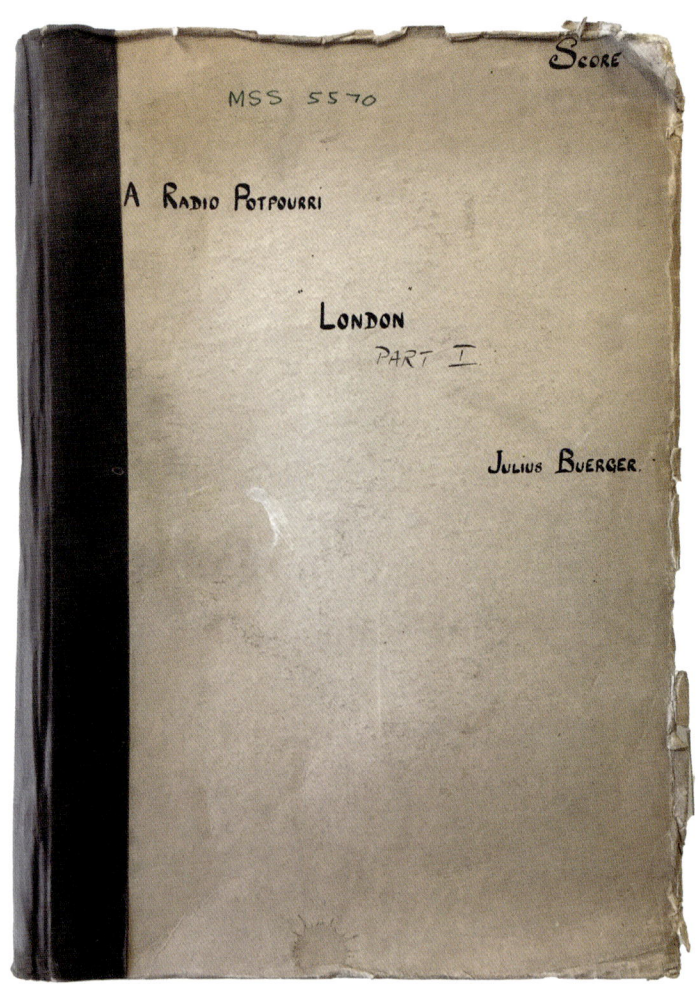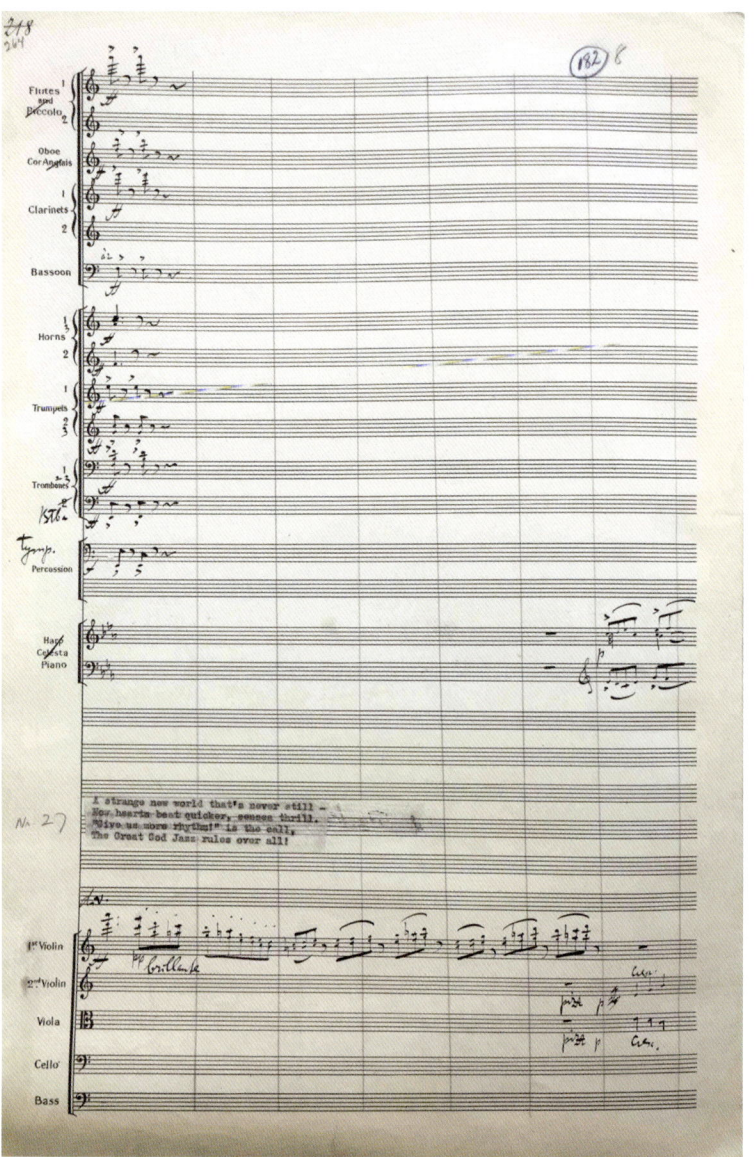

Left: Cover of *Themes of London* (1937) score. Right: An example of the typical narrative dialogue from a Radio Potpourri. This one ushers in a Jazz themed section representing the smoky Jazz clubs and night life of London in late 1930s London. © A-Weaz

fewer than six works and arrangements by émigrés were performed on the BBC in the early to mid-1930s and none on the BBC Home Service during the Second World War.[229] The oversight of Burger's Radio Potpourri is likely due, in this case, to the fact these works have only recently been rediscovered and the scarce research to date on the originator of the Radio Potpourri. At least thirteen Grand potpourri as well as multiple Miniature potpourri, arrangements and orchestrations by Julius Burger were premiered between 1934 and 1945, with the majority being rebroadcast or revived later.

In addition, at least six Radio Potpourri were included into programming on the Home Service from 1939 to 1945. These include *The Empire Sings!* (18 February 1940), *Johann Strauss: A Biography in Music* (19 July 1942, 14 May 1944, 6 August 1944), *Liebestraum* (7 March 1943, 24 September 1944, 25 March 1945), *New World Rhapsody* (3 and 5 March 1944, 20 August 1944), *City of Music* (9 July 1944), and *Life of Offenbach* (3 September 1944, 5 November 1944), with the Victory Rhapsody premiering shortly after VE day (13 and 20 May 1945, 18 November 1945).

The Radio Potpourri serve as a significant contribution to Burger's œuvre and their use in BBC programming in the early stages of the radio broadcasting is noteworthy.

4. CONCLUSION

Julius Burger's storied career as a composer spans the vast majority of the 20th Century and intersected with many important musical figures and institutions of Western Classical music. This ranges from his studies at the with Franz Schreker and Engelbert Humperdinck (Akademie für Musik und darstellende Kunst Wien and Hochschule für Musik Berlin), to his engagements at premiere opera institutions (the Metropolitan Opera and the Kroll Oper Berlin) as well as work in radio (Funkstunde AG Berlin and BBC – London). His works primarily belong to the traditions of early 20th century Austro German with stylistic elements stemming from the likes of Alexander Zemlinsky, Joseph Marx, Franz Schmidt and his former teacher, Franz Schreker. His strong aptitude for arranging also appears to have contributed to the absorption of further musical styles which helped to formulate an idiom which is uniquely his own. These factors, coupled with an impressive array of compositions for many mediums, are sure to garner the attention of musicians and musicologists alike.

---

229 These include Hans Gál's orchestration of Schubert's *Divertissement* (8 November 1939) and Mátyás Seiber's arrangement of *Four Greek Songs* for soprano and string orchestra (1 February 1945) and the remaining four are representative of light music (Ernst Toch's *Bunte Suite* (broadcast 8 January 1934), Fritz Hart's Fantasy – *Cold Blows the Wind* (25 September 1936), Karol Rathaus' *Serenade* (30 October 1936) and suite *The Lion in Love* (13 May 1938). Source: Ibid, p.254.

Julius Burger playing through a score in between performances at the Metropolitan Opera NYC. 1950s. © A-Weaz

ESTATE JULIUS BÜRGER

MS = Manuscript, MS/C = Copyist's Handwriting

1.   **Works**

1.1.   **Instrumental Music**

1.1.1.   **Keyboard**

1.1.1.1.   **Solo Piano**

1.1.1.1.1.   Paganini *[Box 1]*
For Piano Solo
Score Photocopy of MS [incomplete]

1.1.2.   **Chamber Music**

1.1.2.1.   **Duo**

1.1.2.2.   **Arrangement for Duo by Julius Burger**

1.1.2.2.1.   Serenade *[Box 1]*
Music by Antonin Dvořák, op. 85, No. 9
[Version for Violin and Piano; Version for Flute, Oboe, 2 Clarinets, 2 Bassoons and 2 Horns see 1.1.2.5.1.]
Score MS and Violin Part MS

1.1.2.3.   **Trio**

1.1.2.3.1.   Family Serenade *[Box 1]*
composed for the Klein Brothers by Julius Burger
For Flute / Piccolo and 2 Horns
1. Family Idyll
2. Brothers under the Skin
3. Quiet Afternoon at Home
4. Goin' for a Ride
Score MS and Parts MS/C

1.1.2.4.   **Quartet**

1.1.2.4.1.   String Quartet [Nr. 1] (1967) *[Box 1]*
Score. MS [incomplete; only last Page] and Violoncello Part MS

1.1.2.4.2.   String Quartet Nr. 2 (1968) *[Box 1]*
Score. MS and Parts MS

1.1.2.4.3.   String Quartet Nr. 3 (1968) *[Box 2]*
Score MS and Parts MS

1.1.2.4.4.   Adagio. Das letzte Lebewohl (The last Goodbye) (1978) *[Box 2]*
[Version for String Quartet; Version for String Orchestra see 1.1.3.2.3.]
Score MS and Parts MS

1.1.2.5.   **Octet**

1.1.2.5.1.   Serenade *[Box 2]*
Music by Antonin Dvořák, op. 85, No. 9 arranged by Julius Burger
[Version for Flute, Oboe, 2 Clarinets, 2 Bassoons, 2 Horns and Piano; Version for Violin and Piano see 1.1.2.2.1.]
Parts MS

1.1.3.   **Orchestra**

1.1.3.1.   **Solo Instrument and Orchestra**

1.1.3.1.1.   Konzert [Concerto] (1932) *[Box 3, 4, 5]*
For Violoncello and Orchestra
Score MS, Piano Reduction MS and Parts MS/C

1.1.3.1.2. Zigeunerlied [Gypsy Song] (1932) *[Box 6, 7]*
For Violin and Orchestra
[Solo Violin Parts appear in different Versions]
Score MS, Piano Reduction MS and Parts MS/C

1.1.3.2. String Orchestra

1.1.3.2.1. Symphonic Scherzo (1939) *[Box 8, 9]*
For String Orchestra
Score MS and Parts MS

1.1.3.2.2. Theme and Variations *[Box 10]*
For String Orchestra
Score MS and Violoncello Part MS

1.1.3.2.3. Adagio. Das letzte Lebewohl
(The last Goodbye) *[Box 10]*
[Version for String Orchestra; Version for String Quartet see 1.1.2.4.4.]
Score MS and Parts MS/C

1.1.3.3. Arrangement for String Orchestra by Julius Burger

1.1.3.3.1. Three Studies *[Box 10]*
For Piano by F. Chopin arranged for String Orchestra by Julius Burger
1. op. 10, No. 7 (Transposed)
2. op. 10, No. 6 (Transposed)
3. op. 25, No. 9 (Transposed)
Score MS and Parts MS/C

1.1.3.3.2. First Suite of Four Classic Songs *[Box 10]*
arranged for Strings by Julius Burger
Auch kleine Dinge (Hugo Wolf)
Auf dem Wasser zu singen (Franz Schubert)
Mondnacht (Robert Schumann)
Ständchen (Johannes Brahms)
Score MS

1.1.3.3.3. Second Suite Classic Songs *[Box 10]*
arranged for Strings by Julius Burger
Der Jüngling an der Quelle
Der Gärtner (Hugo Wolf)
Freundliche Vision (Richard Strauss)
Vergebliches Ständchen (Johannes Brahms)
Score MS

1.1.3.4. Symphony Orchestra

1.1.3.4.1. Suite of Five Little Pieces from Vienna (1936) *[Box 11]*
For Orchestra
Score MS and Particell MS

1.1.3.4.2. Prelude (1954) *[Box 11]*
For Orchestra
Score Photocopy of MS

1.1.3.4.3. Eastern Symphony *[Box 11, 12, 13]*
For Orchestra
Score MS and Parts MS

1.1.3.4.4. Musical Jest with Johann Strauß *[Box 14]*
For Orchestra
Score MS and Parts MS/C

1.1.3.5. Arrangement for Symphony Orchestra by Julius Burger

1.1.3.5.1. Rondo Capriccioso (1950) *[Box 14]*
Rondo Capriccioso op. 14 by Felix Mendelssohn-Bartholdy arranged for Symphony Orchestra by Julius Burger
Score MS

Romanian Fantasy *[Box 14]*
For Symphony Orchestra arranged by Julius Burger
Particell MS

1.1.3.5.2. Variations on a Theme by Carl Philipp Emanuel Bach *[Box 14, 15, 16]*
arranged for Symphony Orchestra by Julius Burger
Score MS, Piano Reduction MS and Parts MS

1.2. Vocal Music

1.2.1. Voice and Piano

1.2.1.1. Dämmernd liegt der Sommerabend (1915) *[Box 17]*
For Voice and Piano
Text by Heinrich Heine
Score MS

1.2.1.2. Regen (1919) *[Box 17]*
For Voice and Piano
Text by Johannes Schlaf
Score MS and Parts MS/C

1.2.1.3. Seliges Ende (1919) *[Box 17]*
For Voice and Piano
Text by Franz Karl Ginzkey
Score MS

1.2.1.4. Abendläuten (1920) *[Box 17]*
For Voice and Piano
Text by Christian Morgenstern
Score MS and Parts MS/C

1.2.1.5. Lieder im Abend (1926) *[Box 17]*
For Voice and Piano
Text by Hubert von Meyerinck
Score MS

1.2.1.6. Ein Winterabend (1967) *[Box 17]*
For Voice and Piano
Text by Georg Trakl
Score MS

1.2.1.7. Dann (1967) *[Box 17]*
For Voice and Piano
Text by Gottfried Benn
Score MS

1.2.1.8. Liebesgedicht (1967) *[Box 17]*
For Voice and Piano
Text by Ricarda Huch
Score MS

1.2.1.9. Auf eine alte Partitur (1967) *[Box 17]*
For Voice and Piano
Text by Herbert Eulenberg
Score MS

1.2.1.10. Man soll in keiner Stadt... (1968) *[Box 17]*
For Voice and Piano
Text by Klabund
Score MS

1.2.1.11. So tanze meine Seele, vor dem Herrn! (1968) *[Box 17]*
Version for Voice and Piano
[Version for Voice and Orchestra see 1.2.3.1.]
Text by Adolf von Hatzfeld
Score MS

1.2.1.12. Venedig (1970) *[Box 17]*
Version for Voice and Piano
[Version for Voice and Orchestra see 1.2.3.5.]
Text by Friedrich Nietzsche
Score MS

1.2.1.13. Lieder des Alters (1970, 1975) *[Box 17]*
For Voice and Piano
Text by Emanuel Geibel, Mattias Claudius, Johann Wolfgang von Goethe, Music by Julius Burger
Score MS

1.2.1.14. Vier heitere Lieder (1979) [Box 17]
For Voice and Piano
Text by Gotthold Ephraim Lessing
1. Der Irrtum
2. Die Namen
3. Die Schöne von hinten
4. Die Küsse
Score MS

1.2.1.15. Das Staufenlied (1986) [Box 17]
For Voice and Piano
Score Photocopy of MS

1.2.1.16. Nobody (1988) [Box 17]
For Voice and Piano
Text and Music by Julius Burger
Score MS

1.2.1.17. Good-bye, Vienna (1988) [Box 17]
For Voice and Piano
Text and Music by Julius Bürger
Score MS

1.2.1.18. Volkslied [Box 17]
For Voice and Piano
Text by Rainer Maria Rilke
Score MS

1.2.1.19. Schlummerlied [Box 17]
For Voice and Piano
Text by Alfred Mombert
Score MS

1.2.1.20. The Long Furrow [Box 17]
For Voice and Piano
Text by Anne Page
Score MS

1.2.1.21. Über den Bergen und Volkslied [Box 17]
For Voice and Piano
Text „Über den Bergen" by Karl Busse,
Text „Volkslied" by Rainer Maria Rilke
Score MS

1.2.1.22. Hinterm Kornfeld [Box 17]
For Voice and Piano
Text by Carl Hauptmann
Score MS

1.2.1.23. Frühlingsglaube [Box 17]
For Voice and Piano
Text by Gottfried Keller
Score MS

1.2.2. Arrangement for Voice and Piano by Julius Burger

1.2.2.1. Canzona (Cherubino) (196?) [Box 17]
Music from Le Nozze di Figaro by Wolfgang
Amadeus Mozart, Libretto by Lorenza da Ponte,
Cherubino's Aria, Piano Accompaniment
by Julius Burger
Score MS

1.2.2.2. Wiener Blut [Box 17]
Arranged by Julius Bürger for 2 Coloratura
Sopranos and 2 Pianos
English Text by Ruth and Thomas Martin
Score MS

1.2.3. Voice and Orchestra

1.2.3.1. So tanze, meine Seele (1985) [Box 18]
Version for Voice and Orchestra
[Version for Voice and Piano see 1.2.1.11.]
Text by Adolf von Hatzfeld
Score MS

1.2.3.2. Legende [Box 18]
For Bass and Orchestra
Text by Christian Morgenstern
Score MS, Piano Reduction MS and Parts MS/C

1.2.3.3. Stille der Nacht [Box 19]
For Baritone and Orchestra
Text by Gottfried Keller
Score MS and Parts MS/C

1.2.3.4. Schlummerlied [Box 20]
For Voice and Orchestra
Text by Alfred Mombert
Score MS

1.2.3.5. Venedig [Box 20]
[Version for Voice and Orchestra; Version for Voice and Piano see 1.2.1.12.]
[Text by Friedrich Nietzsche]
Score MS

1.2.4. Arrangement for Voice and Orchestra by Julius Burger

1.2.4.1. Verborgenheit [Box 20]
For Voice and Piano by Hugo Wolf, arranged for Voice and Orchestra by Julius Bürger,
Text by Eduard Mörike
Score MS [incomplete, Page 6 is missing]

1.2.4.2. In dem Schatten meiner Locken [Box 20]
For Voice and Piano by Hugo Wolf, arranged for Voice and Orchestra by Julius Bürger,
Text by Paul Heyse
Score MS [incomplete]

1.2.5. Choral Works

1.2.5.1. Mixed Choir with Keyboard

1.2.5.1.1. Service for the Sabbath Morning (CR 1946) [Box 20]
For Cantor, Mixed Choir and Organ
1. Mah town / 2. Bor'chu es Adonoy / 3. Sh'mah / 4. Mi chomocho / 5. Tzur Yisroel / 6. Kedusha / 7. May the Words / 8. S'u sh'orim / 9. Boruch shenosan toroh / 10. Sh'ma Yisroel / 10a. Sh'ma Yisroei / 11. L'cho Adonoy / 12. Gad'lu / 13. Hodo al eretz / 14. Ez chayim / 15. Waanach nu / 16. On that day / 17. En kelohenu / Final Amen
Score MS

1.2.5.1.2. Miserere (1969) [Box 20, 21]
For mixed Choir and Organ
Text by Ferdinand von Saar
Score MS, Organ Reduction MS/C

1.2.5.1.3. Hallelujah [Box 22]
For Mixed Choir and Organ
Score MS

1.2.6. Stage Works

1.2.6.1. Arrangement for Ballet by Julius Burger

1.2.6.1.1. Vittorio (1954) [Box 22]
Ballet in 3 Scenes by Zachary Solov [Dancer and Choreographer]
Music by Giuseppe Verdi, arranged by Julius Burger
Piano Score MS

1.2.7. **Musical Sketches und Other** [Box 22]

1.2.7.1. Sketches to Strauss
Particell + Score Sketches

1.2.7.2. Miscellaneous Sketches [Box 22]
La Bohème by Giacomo Puccini, Aria: Marcello. Finalmente!
En Svane (Grieg, op. 25, No. 2)
For Soprano and Piano, handwritten Copy from the Original Music by Julius Burger
Sketch

1.2.7.3. [Orchestration Study Aids] [Box 22]
Sketch

1.2.7.4. Miscellaneous Music Fragments [Box 22]
Score / Parts Photocopy of MS

1.2.7.5. Fragments of Orchestral Parts from unidentified Work [Box 22]
Parts MS

1.2.7.6. Miscellaneous Music Fragments [Box 22]
Auber / Auguste Franchomine / Canon / Chant Du Gondolier / Enigme / Nocturne / Pensée / Preludio / Romeo and Juliet / [unknown]
Parts MS/C

1.3. **Radio Music**

Common Instrumentation: Narrator, Soloists, Chorus, Symphony Orchestra, Piano, Organ

1.3.1. Life of Jaques Offenbach (1934) [BBC Box 1]
A Life-Story in Music by Julius Bürger,
Dialogues by Dr. Arthur Kulka
[56 Minutes]
Score MS

1.3.2. Holiday in Europe (1934) [BBC Box 1]
idea by Eric Maschwitz, composed and arranged by Julius Burger, Dialogues by Dr. Arthur Kulka
[58 Minutes]
Score MS

1.3.3. A Potpourri of Melodies of Leo Fall (1934) [BBC Box 1]
Composed and Orchestrated by Julius Bürger
Vienna for the British Broadcasting Corporation
[10 Minutes]
Score MS

1.3.4. Potpourri of Melodies by Edmond Audran (1936) [BBC Box 2]
Arranged by Julius Buerger
[9,5-10 Minutes]
Score MS

1.3.5. Potpourri of Schubert Waltzes (1936) [BBC Box 2]
Arranged by Julius Buerger
[12 Minutes]
Score MS

1.3.6. A Festival of Folk Music (1936) [BBC Box 2]
[59 Minutes]
Score MS

1.3.7. The Empire Sings! (1938) [BBC Box 3]
Arranged by Julius Buerger
Score MS

1.3.8. [Sea Shanties from Songs of the British Isles (No. 6) (1938)] [BBC Box 4]
Score MS

1.3.9. New World Rhapsody (1942) [BBC Box 3]
[56 Minutes]
Score MS

1.3.10. Potpourri of Waltzes by Mark H. Lubbock
[BBC Box 4]
Arranged by Julius Bürger
[7:50 Minutes]
Score MS

1.3.11. Archibald Joyce Waltz Potpourri *[BBC Box 4]*
Arranged by Julius Bürger
[10:40 Minutes]
Score MS

1.3.12. Oh No John! *[BBC Box 4]*
In C#, arranged by Julius Bürger
Score MS

1.3.13. Excelsior *[BBC Box 4]*
Music by Michael William Balfe, arranged by Julius Bürger
[5:30 Minutes]
Score MS

1.3.14. Edmund Eysler-Potpourri *[BBC Box 4]*
Arranged by Julius Bürger
[13 Minutes]
Score MS

1.3.15. Star of Bethlehem *[BBC Box 4]*
Music by Stephen Adams, orchestrated by Julius Bürger
[5 Minutes]
Score MS

1.3.16. Homage to Johann Strauss. Strauss Potpourri. Part I *[BBC Box 5]*
A Potpourri by Julius Buerger
[23 Minutes]
Score MS

1.3.17. Homage to Johann Strauss. Strauss Potpourri. Part II *[BBC Box 5]*
A Potpourri by Julius Buerger
Score MS

1.3.18. Come, Dorothy, Come *[BBC Box 5]*
Traditional Swabian Song orchestrated by Julius Bürger
[2:20 Minutes]
Score MS

1.3.19. Selection of Boer War Songs *[BBC Box 5]*
Arranged by Julius Bürger
[7:40 Minutes]
Score MS

1.3.20. Regimental Song from The White Eagle
[BBC Box 5]
Music by Rudolf Friml, orchestrated by Julius Bürger
[2:30 Minutes]
Score MS

1.3.21. Selection of Military Marches *[BBC Box 5]*
Arranged by Julius Bürger
[5 Minutes]
Score MS

1.3.22. Reve Devin *[BBC Box 6]*
Music by Emile Waldteufel, arranged by Julius Bürger
[5:15 Minutes]
Score MS

1.3.23. Asleep in the Deep *[BBC Box 6]*
Music by H.W. Petrie, orchestrated by Julius Bürger
Score MS

1.3.24. London. A Radio Potpourri *[BBC Box 6]*
Score MS

1.3.25. The Little Damozel *[BBC Box 6]*
Music by Ivor Novello, orchestrated by Julius Bürger
Score MS

1.3.26. Bedouin Love Song *[BBC Box 6]*
Music by Puisuti, orchestrated by Julius Bürger
Score MS

PHOTO CREDITS

Archiv des Exilarte Zentrum der mdw – Universität für Musik und darstellende Kunst Wien (A-Weaz)

Archiv der Universität Wien

Brian Coats

Leeds Mercury Newspaper

Radio Times Magazine

Ryan Hugh Ross, private collection

Joseph Schmidt Archiv, Zürich

Julius Bürger CD:
Live Concert August 18th, 2023
ORF RadioKulturhaus
(please contact info@exilarte.org)